AMERICAN INDIAN LIVES

SPIRITUAL LEADERS

• • •

Paul Robert Walker

Facts On File®

AN INFOBASE HOLDINGS COMPANY

On the cover: Black Elk (left); Ruby Modesto (right)

Spiritual Leaders

Copyright © 1994 by Paul Robert Walker

Facts On File, Inc.
460 Park Avenue South
New York NY 10016

Library of Congress Cataloging-in-Publication Data

Walker, Paul Robert.
  Spiritual leaders / Paul Robert Walker.
    p. cm. — (American Indian lives)
  Includes bibliographical references and index.
  ISBN 0-8160-2875-3
    1. Indians of North America—Religion and mythology—Juvenile
literature.   2. Indians of North America—Biography—Juvenile
literature.   3. Prophets—North America—Biography—Juvenile
literature.   4. Shamans—North America—Biography—Juvenile
literature.   [1. Indians of North America—Religion and mythology.
  2. Indians of North America—Biography.]   I. Title. II. Series: American
Indian lives (New York, N.Y.)
  E98.R3W35   1994
  299'.7—dc20   93-31684

A British CIP catalogue record for this book is available from the British
Library.

Text design by Ellen Levine
Cover design by Nora Wertz
Composition by Grace M. Ferrara\Facts On File, Inc.
Manufactured by the Maple-Vail Book Manufacturing Group
Printed in the United States of America

10 9 8 7 6 5 4 3 2 1

This book is printed on acid-free paper.

By Paul Robert Walker

Big Men, Big Country: A Collection of American Tall Tales
Illustrated fiction for young readers

Head for the Hills! The Amazing True Story of the Johnstown Flood
Nonfiction for young readers (Read It to Believe It! series)

The Sluggers Club: A Sports Mystery
A middle-grade novel

Bigfoot and Other Legendary Creatures
Illustrated fiction/nonfiction for young readers

Great Figures of the Wild West
Biographies for young adults (American Profiles series)

The Method
A young adult novel

Pride of Puerto Rico: The Story of Roberto Clemente
Biography for young readers

To the American Indian people, in hopes that a new generation will understand the greatness and importance of your spiritual path.

To Laurie, Matthew, and Colin—seekers on their own spiritual path.

◆ ◆ ◆

CONTENTS

◆ ◆ ◆

ACKNOWLEDGMENTS

◆ ◆ ◆

As with any collection of biographical profiles, I am indebted to the work of many scholars who have studied these leaders in far more detail than I. Their names appear with their works in the Annotated Bibliography.

I owe special thanks to four scholars who read specific profiles and patiently shared their research and insights with me in long letters and longer telephone conversations: Clifford E. Trafzer (Introduction/Smohalla), Joseph B. Herring (Kenekuk), Nancy O. Lurie (Mountain Wolf Woman), and Guy Mount (Ruby Modesto). Although I used their books as sources, their personal input was invaluable, both in clarifying and expanding the material in their books and in correcting my own errors of interpretation. Of course, any errors that remain are mine and mine alone.

Finally, I would like to thank my editor, Nicole Bowen, who has been a pillar of understanding throughout a long and sometimes difficult project. She is not only a fine editor, but as a person of Seneca heritage she brings a sensitivity to the subject that is very helpful to me—a white writer trying to understand and portray a great people who have been too long maligned and misunderstood.

INTRODUCTION

◆ ◆ ◆

In 1492, when Christopher Columbus "discovered" America, there were over 10 million native people living on the North American continent. These people belonged to many different tribes, and each tribe had its own religious beliefs and rituals. Thus it is difficult to discuss American Indian religion in general, just as it would be difficult to discuss "white religion." However, certain basic spiritual ideas were found among almost all American Indian tribes.

(Although we discuss these ideas as they existed in the past, American Indian religion is very much alive today—and most of what was true in the past is still true in the present.)

Most tribes believed in a Creator or Supreme Being. They considered the earth to be sacred and believed that certain plants, animals, objects, songs, and dances were sacred as well. They believed in the power of visions and dreams, and considered them just as real—or more real—than the experiences of everyday life. Instead of looking for spiritual truth in a book like the Bible, the Indians experienced spiritual truth directly in their visions and dreams.

But perhaps the most basic spiritual truth among American Indian tribes is this: Religion was an integral and essential part of their daily lives. They did not go to church on Sunday morning and then forget about it the rest of the week. Every action—from household chores to politics, hunting, and warfare—had spiritual significance. In *American Indian Prophets*, historian Clifford E. Trafzer expresses this simply and eloquently: "Religion was the heart of the Indian community."

With the great importance of religion in their daily lives, the

Indian people have always had great respect for their spiritual leaders. These leaders often gained their spiritual power directly through their visions or as gifts from the Creator, as well as through the teachings of older leaders. Depending upon their specific visions, gifts, or training, Indian spiritual leaders might cure illness, perform sacred ceremonies, control the weather, find lost objects, predict the future, or conduct prayers and rituals for the well-being of an individual or the tribe.

Each tribe had its own name for spiritual leaders, and some tribes had different names for leaders with different powers. Historians and anthropologists have generally used three different terms for these leaders: *shaman*, *medicine man* (or woman), and *Indian doctor*. Although there are slight differences in the original meanings of these terms, they all refer to individuals who possess spiritual power.

Unfortunately, white people also called Indian spiritual leaders by many disrespectful names: fakes, frauds, imposters, charlatans, magicians, witch doctors, and devil worshippers. This reflects a lack of understanding of Indian culture and Indian religion. It also reflects an attitude that the only "right" religion is Christianity. Ironically, the missionaries and most other whites who denounced the wonders performed by Indian spiritual leaders as fakery were perfectly willing to believe in the miracles of Jesus or the Hebrew Prophets.

As with other aspects of Indian-white relations, the American Indians were more generous and open-minded toward Christianity than the whites were toward Indian religion. The Indians were genuinely interested in the ideas taught by the missionaries, and many were willing to accept Christianity as a good road for the whites and perhaps even a good road for some Indians—as long as they could also keep their traditional beliefs. However, most Christian missionaries refused to accept this combination of ideas, viewing all Indian religion as "pagan idolatry" or "devil worship."

The Lakota holy man Black Elk explained this hypocrisy very well. "The whites think we have the power from the devil," he said, "but I'll say that they probably have that themselves . . . They take everything we have just gradually until we won't have anything left."

Even whites who could see the greatness and nobility of Indian chiefs and military leaders could not understand the importance of Indian spiritual leaders. This contrast is clear in the writings of Samuel Gardner Drake, an early 19th-century historian who was generally sympathetic and respectful toward the Indians.

In *The Book of the Indians*, Drake wrote many glowing pages about the Seneca chief Cornplanter, calling him "venerable" and pointing out that he "was very early distinguished for his wisdom in council." But Drake dismissed Cornplanter's half-brother, Handsome Lake, in two sentences: "[Handsome Lake], commonly called the Prophet, was brother to Corn-Plant and resided in his village. He was of little note, and died previous to 1816." Yet it was Handsome Lake, the Prophet of the Good Word, who gave new life to his people and started a religion that is still practiced today.

Similarly, Drake referred to the Shawnee leader Tecumseh as "this persevering and extraordinary man," but he dismissed Tecumseh's brother, Tenskwatawa, the Shawnee Prophet, as "that famous imposter." Yet it was the visions and teachings of Tenskwatawa that formed the spiritual basis of Tecumseh's political power.

For non-Indians, the turning point in understanding the importance of Indian spiritual leaders occurred at the end of the 19th century. In late 1890, a white anthropologist named James Mooney was sent by the Bureau of Ethnology to investigate the Ghost Dance, a powerful Indian religious movement that had swept across the Plains that year.

Mooney discovered that the Ghost Dance was an extraordinary, complex system of spiritual beliefs and ceremonies that varied from tribe to tribe. He also realized that the Ghost Dance was only the most recent in a long series of Indian spiritual movements that had developed in response to pressure from the white invaders. Modern scholars call these "revitalization movements" because they brought new life to their people as their traditional culture was slowly being destroyed by the whites.

Mooney's report, published in 1896, was the first book that discussed Indian spiritual leaders and their teachings with genuine respect. However, it was not until the second half of the 20th century that a significant number of scholars began to study these leaders seriously. By that time the leaders themselves were long dead, as were most of their followers. But through careful research, historians and anthropologists have been able to piece together many aspects of their lives and teachings.

Of the 13 leaders profiled in this book, eight led revitalization movements. These leaders are usually called Prophets, because they spoke of a better world to come and led their people through times of crisis, just like the great spiritual leaders of the Old Testament.

There is great variety in the lives and spiritual teachings of these Prophets. Popé, the Prophet of the Pueblo Revolt, completely rejected all European influences while advocating a return to traditional Pueblo religion and culture. John Slocum, the Shaker Prophet, rejected some traditional Indian religious practices while adopting many Christian ideas. Tenskwatawa, the Shawnee Prophet, preached war against the whites, while Kenekuk, the Kickapoo Prophet, preached peace. But despite their diversity, all these Prophets gained spiritual power through visions and tried to use that power to lead their people toward a better way of life.

The other five profiles reflect various aspects of Indian spiritual leadership. Passaconaway, the first leader profiled in the book, was a medicine man who used his spiritual power to attain political leadership. In this sense, he is similar to more famous Indian leaders like Sitting Bull, Crazy Horse, and Geronimo—all of whom were spiritual leaders as well as military and political leaders. White officials never understood this strong connection between spiritual power and secular power among the Indians. In fact, when they wanted to deny Sitting Bull's leadership, they called him "just a medicine man," not realizing that his role as a medicine man was an important part of his role as a chief. The same can be said of Passaconaway.

The lives of Zotom and Black Elk reflect the pull between traditional Indian religion on one hand and Christianity on the other. After being imprisoned as a Kiowa warrior, Zotom became an Episcopal minister and struggled to convert his fellow tribespeople. However, he never found satisfaction in orthodox Christianity and ultimately turned to the peyote religion, which combines Christian ideas with traditional Indian beliefs and ceremonies.

Black Elk's life developed in the opposite direction. After an extraordinary childhood vision, he became a traditional Lakota medicine man. Then, in his early forties, he converted to the Catholic religion and spent the rest of his long life as a practicing Christian. However, he never forgot the spiritual path of his younger days and helped preserve Lakota religion in three books, including the famous *Black Elk Speaks*.

The last two leaders profiled, Mountain Wolf Woman and Ruby Modesto, reflect the role of women in Indian spiritual leadership. Although many tribes accepted women as visionaries and healers, non-Indians knew little about American Indian women until the 20th century. There are two reasons for this. First, while some tribal groups were matriarchal, most Indian tribes have been dominated by men just as white society has been male-dominated. Second, the early white explorers, soldiers, missionaries, and anthropologists were almost exclusively men, and they generally reported on the role of Indian men.

Fortunately, this male emphasis has begun to change, and we now have the fascinating life stories of Mountain Wolf Woman and Ruby Modesto, along with stories of other Indian women. Like Zotom, Mountain Wolf Woman was a spiritual seeker who experienced traditional Indian religion and white Christianity before finding satisfaction in the unique Indian-style Christianity of the peyote religion. Ruby Modesto also experienced white Christianity, but ultimately found her own path as a traditional shaman, practicing spiritual healing into the late 20th century.

The 13 profiles cover almost 400 years of North American history, stretching across the continent from 17th-century New England to 20th-century southern California. The profiles emphasize the lives of the leaders themselves, and each profile is designed to stand alone. However, together these 13 lives tell a greater and more disturbing story: the white invasion of North America and the efforts of Indian spiritual leaders to help their people cope with the destruction of their traditional way of life.

Although the book ends with the death of Ruby Modesto in

1980, Indian spiritual leaders continue to help their people face the realities of the modern world. In late spring 1993, just as this manuscript was nearing completion, a mysterious and deadly virus spread across the Navajo Reservation in Arizona and New Mexico. At least 11 young and apparently healthy people died of sudden respiratory failure. While public health officials used modern scientific methods to investigate the illness, two Navajo medicine men performed a sacred ceremony to discover the cause and find a cure.

One of these medicine men, Johnny Barbone, discussed the ideas behind the healing ceremony. "We the *Dineh* people, the earth people, we respect our mother earth. We respect our heavenly father. If you're not in tune with the universe . . . there's sickness in the heart or in the mind . . . We're going to gaze into the hot ash. That will tell us what prayers to use, and if there's any song that needs to be sung."

The next day, state health officials revealed that they had made a breakthrough in discovering the cause of the illness. No one will ever know what part the traditional ceremony of the medicine men played in this scientific breakthrough, but to the Navajo people the two approaches work hand in hand. "They're both extremely important," a tribal spokeswoman explained. "This is a concentrated effort to use every source available—including the spiritual source—to tap in and find a cure. The Navajo have . . . a profound belief in nature and the power of the earth."

Although she was speaking specifically of the Navajo, the same could be said of all American Indian tribes. And this respect for the earth—this spiritual connection to the world that gives us life—is something that non-Indians must learn from the Indian people before it's too late.

PASSACONAWAY

◆ ◆ ◆

Son of the Bear

When the Pilgrims landed at Plymouth in 1620, they found surprisingly few Indians living in the area that became known as New England. Instead they encountered human skeletons littering the countryside. From 1616 to 1619, a terrible sickness had swept through the New England area, killing three-fourths of the native population. This epidemic—which may have been measles, small-pox, or bubonic plague—was brought to the New World by European fishermen.

The epidemic made it much easier for the English to take control of New England. Ten years later, after a second English colony had been established at Massachusetts Bay, Governor John Winthrop commented that the native people were "neere all dead, so as the Lord hath cleared our title to what we possess."

Even before this horrible disaster, the bands and tribes of New England had often united into larger groups called confederacies, with each confederacy ruled by a powerful leader called a grand sachem. After the epidemic, these confederacies became more important, uniting the survivors of many different bands and tribes.

Around 1619 the people who lived along the Merrimack River in what is now New Hampshire and northern Massachusetts united under a grand sachem named Passaconaway, which means "bear cub" or "son of the bear." Passaconaway's people are usually referred to as the Penacook Confederacy or the Pawtuckett Confederacy. Actually these were the names of two villages located at the present sites of Concord, New Hampshire (Penacook) and Lowell, Massachusetts (Pawtuckett). Most of the people under Passaconaway's control belonged to the Western Abnaki and Massachuset tribes.

Passaconaway was a *powah*, or medicine man, who began his career as a spiritual leader and later became a political leader. He was considered a great wonder-worker by his people. It was said that he could make water burn and trees dance; that he could turn himself into a flame; that he could raise a green leaf in the middle of winter and bring a living snake from the skin of a dead snake.

These feats sound like the tricks of a great magician—and Passaconaway probably was an expert in the art of magic. But if magic was the key to Passaconaway's original power, he proved himself to be much more than a magician once he became grand sachem. Under his leadership, the Penacook Confederacy drove the warlike Mohawk from the Merrimack Valley. Then, when faced with the superior military might of the English colonists, Passaconaway turned diplomat and guided his people on the path of peace.

Passaconaway first encountered the English around 1630. At that time he was already an older man, probably in his sixties. Passaconaway later said that he tried all his powers of magic to stop the white-skinned newcomers from taking control of the land. But instead of driving the whites away, he had visions of the English conquest of North America. He saw that resistance was hopeless and would only lead to the destruction of his people.

In 1633 Governor Winthrop of Massachusetts reported that an Englishman had been killed in the lodge of one of Passaconaway's men. The killer escaped with the Englishman's goods, but Passaconaway had the man brought back for punishment—a clear sign of his friendly intentions toward the English.

Almost 10 years later, in 1642, a great fear arose among the English colonists that the Indians were planning to attack. The leaders of Massachusetts decided to take all guns away from the local Indians and sent 40 armed men to Passaconaway's village. It was a very rainy day, and they could not reach the grand sachem's lodge, which was located on an island in the Merrimack River. Instead the men kidnapped Passaconaway's son, Wannalancet, as well as Wannalancet's wife and baby boy.

The Englishmen decided to release the mother and child, and the young woman fled into the forest in fear. She remained in

Passaconaway, Son of the Bear, wearing a bearskin over his shoulders. The origin of this drawing is unknown. Although apparently quite old, it probably does not represent Passaconaway's actual appearance.

hiding for 10 days before returning to Passaconaway's village. In the meantime, the English led Wannalancet away with his hands tied behind his back and a noose around his neck. The men were afraid of Wannalancet because they had been told that he had the same magical powers as his father.

Apparently Wannalancet really did have some unusual powers. On the way to Boston he slipped out of his bonds and escaped into the forest. One of the Englishmen shot at him and narrowly missed. When the Massachusetts leaders heard of this incident, they sent another sachem to Passaconaway with their apologies and explanations—one of the few times in American history that the white invaders apologized for their treatment of the Indians.

Passaconaway refused to deal with the English until his son, daughter-in-law, and grandson were returned. After they all emerged from the forest unharmed, he sent Wannalancet to Boston, where he surrendered their guns and submitted to the questions of the English authorities. When the English were satisfied that the Penacook were not involved in a rebellion, the guns were returned.

Up to this point, Passaconaway had been able to live in friendship with the English while maintaining his own independence. In 1644, however, he appeared before the Massachusetts Court and swore his loyalty to the Colony of Massachusetts. Other New England sachems did the same in response to pressure from the English colonists.

A few years later a Christian missionary named John Eliot visited Passaconaway. At first the grand sachem was hostile toward Eliot and his new religion. But after listening to the white man preach in one of the local Indian dialects, Passaconaway became friendlier. According to Eliot, the grand sachem "gave up himself and his sonnes to pray onto God."

Although Passaconaway was willing to pray to the Christian God, he was not ready to accept Christianity as the right religion for his people. He asked the missionary to stay longer among his people and take the time to explain and prove his teachings.

"What you throw among us is very beautiful," he said, "but we can't look inside. In it may be something or nothing, a stick or stone or precious treasure. If you will [live] among us, we may come to believe that what is inside is all good as you say."

Eliot explained that his first duty was to another group of Indians who had already accepted the gospel. However, the Christian missionary visited the Merrimack villages regularly and remained on good terms with the grand sachem. More than 10 years later, around 1660, Eliot was present when Passaconaway made his farewell speech to his people. The grand sachem was almost 100 years old. According to John Eliot, this is what he said:

> I am now going the way of all flesh, or ready to die, and not likely to see you ever met together any more. I will now leave this word of counsel with you, that you take heed how you quarrel with the English. For though you may do them much mischief, yet assuredly you will all be destroyed, and rooted off the earth if you do . . . I was as much an enemy to the English at their first coming to these parts as anyone whatsoever, and did try all ways and means to have destroyed them, at least to have prevented them sitting down here, but I could in no way effect it; therefore I advise you never to contend with the English, nor make war with them.

Sometime after this speech Passaconaway died, and his son Wannalancet became the grand sachem of the Penacook. True to his father's advice, Wannalancet maintained peaceful relations with the English. When New England became a bloody battleground in the conflict known as King Philip's War (1675–76), Wannalancet and his followers retreated into the woods to avoid the fighting.

No one knows the exact date or place of Passaconaway's death. But there is an old New England folktale that shows how deeply he was honored by his people.

According to this tale, Passaconaway—son of the bear—wrapped himself in a bearskin and sat in a great sled pulled by giant wolves. Singing in spiritual joy, he rode over the snow-covered hills and valleys of New Hampshire and up the steep slope of Mount Washington—the highest point in the White Mountains. As Passaconaway reached the peak, his great sled burst into flames, flew into the sky, and disappeared into the clouds.

POPÉ

◆ ◆ ◆

Prophet of the Pueblo Revolt

In 1540 the Spanish explorer Francisco de Coronado led an expedition from Mexico into what is now the southwestern United States. Coronado was looking for the Seven Cities of Cíbola—a legendary land of golden riches. But instead of gold, he found a highly developed native culture, the culture known as the Pueblo Indians.

When Coronado arrived, the Pueblo lived in about 80 permanent villages in what is now New Mexico and Arizona. Most of these villages were clustered along the upper Rio Grande River, near the present-day cities of Albuquerque and Santa Fe. The Pueblo lived in multistory apartment-style houses built of adobe or stone. These sophisticated structures made a strong impression on the early Spanish explorers, and the name *Pueblo* is the Spanish word for "village" or "town."

After traveling for two years without finding gold, Coronado returned to Mexico in disappointment. For the next 50 years the Pueblo were left to live their traditional lives. They grew corn, beans, squash, cotton, and tobacco. They worshipped their gods with ceremonial dances. They fought only to defend their villages from neighboring tribes such as the Apache and Navajo.

Then in 1592 a new Spanish expedition arrived. This time the Spaniards were not just passing through—they had come to stay. Governor Don Juan de Oñate established the Spanish colony of New Mexico with 130 families, 270 single men, 11 Franciscan priests, around 100 servants, and 7,000 animals. The Spanish colonists had two main goals in New Mexico: to get rich and to save the souls of the "pagan" Indians. Unfortunately, both of these goals made life miserable for the Pueblo people.

Since there was no gold to be found, the only road to riches was to sell slaves or work the land. Many Pueblo—as well as many Apache and Navajo—were captured and sold as slaves in Mexico. However, most of the Pueblo were forced into a more subtle kind of slavery working the land.

The Spanish established a system called the *encomienda* that was similar to the feudal system in Europe. Each year the Pueblo were required to pay taxes of crops and other goods to the Spanish colonists. They were also required to work on the Spanish lands while still maintaining their own fields. In return, the Spanish protected the Pueblo from attacks by other tribes. Although the Pueblo were excellent farmers, this system made it very difficult for them to survive.

If the Spanish colonists were hard on the bodies of the Pueblo, the Spanish priests were even harder on their souls. The Pueblo are extremely religious people, and their religious practices form an important part of their daily life. Pueblo religion emphasizes ceremonial dances to bring rain for the crops and well-being for the village. Some of these dances use masks and dolls that represent supernatural beings called *kachinas*. The Pueblo "church" is a ceremonial chamber called a *kiva*.

The Spanish priests were not interested in Pueblo religion; they wanted to save the Indians' "pagan" souls and turn them into good Christians. Backed by Spanish soldiers, the priests baptized the Pueblo and forced them to attend mass. They destroyed the kivas, burned the kachinas, and punished those who participated in traditional dances.

Outwardly most Pueblo cooperated with the Spanish and pretended to become Christians, but they did not give up their own religion. Instead they continued their dances and ceremonies in secret. And as they danced and prayed to their ancient gods, the Pueblo held onto a single dream: someday they would drive the Spanish from their land and return to their traditional way of life.

In 1675 the governor of New Mexico, Juan Treviño, ordered the arrest of 47 Pueblo religious leaders under accusations of witchcraft and sorcery. The immediate cause of the arrests was the death of a sickly Franciscan priest and a number of other deaths among the Spanish. Supposedly the Pueblo medicine men had "bewitched" the victims. In fact the arrests were part of the continuing efforts by the Spanish to destroy Pueblo religion.

All of the medicine men were whipped and tortured, and three were hanged as an example. A fourth allegedly hanged himself. While the surviving religious leaders waited in prison, a group of 70 armed Pueblos appeared at the governor's villa in Santa Fe and demanded that he release the medicine men. The 70 Pueblos were reenforced by hundreds of others waiting in the surrounding hills. Faced with the possibility of an attack on the capital, Governor Treviño released the medicine men.

One of the released prisoners was a medicine man from San Juan Pueblo named Po'png, which means "Pumpkin Mountain" in Tewa—one of the Pueblo languages. Po'png was called "Popé" by the Spanish. At the time of his release, Popé was already an old man. He had lived his whole life under the harsh hand of Spanish rule and burned with hatred for the white-skinned oppressors. Now the time had come to take action.

Popé announced that he had journeyed to the far northern lake of Shibapu, where the Pueblo people first stepped onto the earth. There he met the kachinas, who gave him supernatural powers and told him to lead the Pueblo against the foreigners. According to some stories, Popé smeared his body with a magic powder that made him glow like fire as he spoke.

Popé began to sow the seeds of rebellion in his native pueblo of San Juan. He held traditional dances and issued threats against the Spanish. But San Juan was closely watched by the Spanish authorities, so Popé moved on to Taos, the northernmost pueblo in the rugged Sangre de Cristo mountains. There in the kiva of Taos, he continued to hold traditional religious ceremonies and plot the rebellion.

The Pueblo are not a single tribe; they do not even speak a single language. Because of this it has always been difficult for the

The Taos Pueblo, where Popé plotted the Pueblo Revolt.   (Library of Congress)

villages to work together. However, sparked by Popé, the Pueblo united against their common enemy. Leaders from almost every village agreed to participate in the rebellion. Secrecy was essential, and Popé himself was ruthless in pursuing his dream. When he suspected that his son-in-law planned to betray the rebels, Popé ordered him stoned to death.

In the summer of 1680, Popé and the other leaders sent out two messengers carrying knotted cords of plant fiber. The knotted cord was a traditional Pueblo way of counting, but these cords had a special meaning: each knot represented a day before the great rebellion. When all the knots were untied, the time of the rebellion had come. Some historians believe that the messengers actually carried two different sets of cords. The cords indicating the true date of the rebellion were given to leaders trusted by Popé and the other plotters, while cords indicating a later date were given to those who were not trusted.

The rebellion was originally scheduled for August 11, the night of the new moon. However, despite all the efforts at secrecy, some Christian Pueblos betrayed the plans to their local priests, and the priests informed Governor Antonio de Otermín. On August 9 the governor sent soldiers to the pueblo of Tesuque, where they captured the two messengers and brought them back to Santa Fe for questioning. News of the betrayal quickly reached Popé and the other leaders, who decided that the rebellion should begin immediately.

That evening the people of Tesuque killed a Spanish trader in anger over the capture of the messengers. Fearing for his own safety, the village priest, Father Juan Pío, decided to spend the night in Santa Fe. When he returned the next morning to say mass, he found Tesuque deserted and the people waiting in the nearby hills. The men had painted their faces red, and they carried weapons in their hands.

Father Pío approached his former flock and tried to plead for peace. "What is this, children; are you mad? Do not disturb yourselves; I will help you and die a thousand deaths for you."

But the time for peace was past. The warriors of Tesuque killed Father Pío in a ravine. Then they moved on to the church, demolished the religious statues, and burned the building to the ground. The Pueblo Revolt had begun.

During the next few days, 400 Spanish colonists—including 21 Franciscan friars—were killed by the Pueblo. Governor Otermín took refuge behind the walls of Santa Fe with a thousand colonists and servants. For five days the Pueblo surrounded the capital, cutting off the water supply. Faced with slow death by thirst, Governor Otermín decided to attack.

In a bloody all-day battle, the Spanish drove the Pueblo back and killed almost 300 Indians while losing only a handful of their own men. But even this success was not enough to save the colony. The next day Otermín led his colonists out of the capital on a long march of retreat. The Pueblo warriors allowed them to pass in safety. They did not really want to kill the Spanish. They just wanted them to leave.

About 70 miles to the south, Lieutenant General Alonso García had taken refuge with 1,500 colonists in the pueblo of Isleta. At first the people of Isleta refused to fight the Spanish, but as the days passed, more and more Isletans joined the rebellion. Faced with a lack of supplies and the threat of attack, García's followers also decided to abandon the colony. Colonists led by Otermín and García met in southern New Mexico and continued on to what is now El Paso, Texas. The revolt was a brilliant success. There were no more Spaniards in the land of the Pueblo.

There is some disagreement about Popé's role in the Pueblo Revolt. The Spanish identified him as the supreme leader, and most non-Indian historians have gone along with this. However, Pueblo historians believe that Popé was just one of many leaders. Joe S. Sando—a native of Jemez Pueblo—wrote: " . . . as in most Pueblo endeavors, there were representatives from each village who helped plan and execute the revolt."

Whatever his exact role in plotting the rebellion, Popé emerged as the new leader of the Pueblo. Acting under his orders, the Pueblo wiped out all traces of Christianity. "The god of the Christians is dead," Popé proclaimed. "He was made of rotten wood."

Churches that survived the rebellion were destroyed in the first days of freedom. Wooden crosses and statues of the saints crackled in bonfires throughout the villages. Pueblo who had been baptized by the Spanish priests purified themselves with a special soap. Christian marriages were declared invalid, and men were encouraged to take new wives. Speaking Spanish or the names of Jesus and Mary was punishable by death. The ceremonial Pueblo dances were once again held in complete freedom.

Along with Christianity, Popé tried to wipe out all traces of Spanish culture. The Pueblo killed Spanish cattle, uprooted fruit trees, and grew nothing but native plants in their fields. They released Spanish horses from their corrals, allowing them to run free until captured by the more warlike Indians of the Plains. The Plains Indians already had some Spanish horses from earlier contact with the Pueblo, but the release of the Spanish herds was an important turning point in the horse culture that flourished on the Plains for the next two centuries.

To ensure obedience Popé toured the pueblos in regal style, riding on a black mule, dressed in a traditional costume, and wearing a bull's horn strapped to his forehead. Although the people cooperated at first, Popé soon encountered resistance. It was one thing for the villages to unite against the Spanish; but now that the Spanish were gone many people wanted to return to the old ways of independence for each pueblo.

Popé refused to give up his newfound power. He began to act like the old Spanish governors, moving into the governor's villa in Santa Fe and demanding high taxes from the people. He killed his enemies and took women for himself and his supporters.

In the winter of 1681–82, the Pueblo were still united enough to drive away a new expedition by Governor Otermín. As the years passed, however, the united strength of the Pueblo began to weaken. Part of this weakening can be blamed on Popé's unreasonable governing policies, but there were other causes as well.

Although Popé prophesied a time of great prosperity, the weather did not cooperate. Instead, a severe drought created a terrible famine. It was difficult enough to farm the semiarid land during the rainy years, but during dry years it was almost impossible. At the same time, raiders from the Apache, Navajo, and Ute tribes stole whatever food was left. The Spanish had been cruel masters, but at least their guns had kept the raiders away from the Pueblo villages.

Popé was overthrown sometime after the revolt and then re-elected as leader in 1688. He died around 1690. Two years later a new Spanish governor, Diego de Vargas, led an expedition into the land of the Pueblo and was welcomed peacefully in most of the villages. The following year Vargas returned to reestablish the colony of New Mexico.

After several years of scattered fighting, the Pueblo ultimately accepted the Spanish as neighbors. For their part, the Spanish improved their treatment of the Pueblo. There was no encomienda system, and the Spanish priests were more tolerant of traditional Pueblo religion.

Today the Pueblo people still live in some of their ancient villages. Although they have adopted many Spanish and American customs, they preserve their traditional way of life and religion. This reflects the strength of the Pueblo people as a whole and the richness of their culture. But at least part of the credit must go to Popé, the medicine man who led the great rebellion more than three centuries ago.

Although he later became a tyrant, Popé was a spiritual leader of great vision—a man who desperately wanted to preserve the traditional life of his people. And the Pueblo Revolt that grew out of his vision was the most successful uprising in the history of the American Indians.

NEOLIN

◆ ◆ ◆

The Delaware Prophet

From 1754 to 1763, France and England fought a series of battles for control of North America. This conflict is often called the French and Indian War because most of the Indian tribes in the Great Lakes and Ohio River regions sided with the French against the British.

At first the French-Indian alliance was too strong for the British forces. But in 1758 the tide of battle turned with new reinforcements from England. The British conquered Canada by 1760, and the French abandoned their forts in the Great Lakes region the following year. Although the peace treaty was not signed until 1763, it was clear that the French had lost the war for North America.

The defeat of the French caused great concern among the Indians who had fought beside them. The French had treated the Indians as equals and allies. They gave gifts to the chiefs in return for their support, and they were more interested in trading than in establishing large settlements. The French fur traders married Indian women, lived in Indian villages, and participated in Indian dances. The French priests impressed the Indians with their courage and showed respect for the Indian way of life.

The English were different. They considered themselves superior to the Indians, and they established large settlements wherever they went. To make matters worse—the head of the

British forces in North America, Lord Jeffrey Amherst, hated Indians with a passion.

Amherst believed that the Indians should be controlled by strict rules and military force, rather than diplomacy and gifts—which he called bribes. Amherst did not understand that the Indians considered such gifts a sign of respect. He also did not understand that the gifts, which included guns and powder for hunting, had become necessary for the Indians' survival.

In this atmosphere of change and uncertainty, a new spiritual leader emerged among the Indians of the Great Lakes region. He is called the Delaware Prophet because he was a member of the Delaware, a tribe that lived along the southern shore of Lake Erie. He is also sometimes called Neolin, which means "the enlightened one."

Around 1762 the Delaware Prophet began preaching in the village of Tuscarawas on the Muskingum River in what is now Ohio. He called for a union of all the Indian tribes and a return to the traditional Indian way of life. The Prophet claimed that he had received his instructions in a great vision. Many details of this vision were recorded in an old French manuscript. Although it does not tell the story in his own words, historians believe the manuscript provides a fair account of the Delaware Prophet's spiritual journey.

Searching to understand the cause of his people's problems, the Prophet decided to seek a divine being called the Master of Life. He set out on his journey carrying his gun, his ammunition, and his cooking kettle. After eight days he came to a place where there were three wide paths. To his amazement, he noticed that the paths grew brighter as the night grew darker. Although he was afraid, he decided that one of these paths must lead to the Master of Life.

The Prophet took the widest path first, but he was driven back by a great fire that burned out of the earth. He then took the next-widest path, but was again driven back by a great fire. Finally he took the narrowest path.

After a day of traveling, he came upon a mountain that blazed with light. At first he could find no way to climb the mountain, but then he noticed a beautiful woman wearing snow-white clothing. She told him that the Master of Life lived on top of the mountain, but that before the Prophet could climb the mountain, he must leave all his clothes and equipment and must wash in a special river.

The Prophet did as the woman ordered, and climbed naked up the slippery side of the mountain. When he reached the top, the woman disappeared and he found himself gazing at three great villages. He walked toward the largest village and was allowed inside the gate. There he met a handsome man, also dressed in white, who led him to the Master of Life.

The Master took the Prophet by the hand and invited him to sit on a hat with a golden border. "I am the Master of Life," he explained, "whom you wish to see and with whom you wish to speak. Listen to what I shall tell you for yourself and all the Indians."

The Master of Life said that the Indians were suffering because they had become wicked. He ordered them to live together in peace, to give up drunkenness, to take only one wife, and to stop singing the medicine song—which he considered a call to the evil spirit. He emphasized that they must stop depending on the whites for food and supplies:

> The land on which you are, I have made for you, not for others. Wherefore do you suffer the whites to dwell upon your lands? Can you not do without them? I know that [the French] supply your wants; but were you not wicked as you are you would not need them. You might live as you did before you knew them . . . did not your bow and arrow maintain you? You needed neither gun, powder, nor any other object.

Although the Master of Life ordered the Indians to stop using the manufactured goods of the French, he said that the French traders could remain among the tribes as friends. At least this is the story according to the French manuscript; some scholars believe that the Prophet actually spoke out against all whites.

Whatever his attitude toward the French, the Master of Life's attitude toward the English was clear:

> Drive from your lands those dogs in red clothing; they are only an injury to you . . . Drive them away; wage war against them; I love

them not; they know me not; they are my enemies; they are your
brother's enemies. Send them back to the lands I have made for
them. Let them remain there.

Finally, the Master of Life gave the Prophet a prayer carved in
Indian symbols on a wooden stick. He ordered the Indians to
repeat the prayer morning and evening. The Prophet promised to
do all that the Master of Life required and to tell others to do the
same. He was then guided down the mountain, where he put on
his clothes and walked back to his village.

After his great vision the Delaware Prophet began to preach
throughout the Great Lakes region. In order to illustrate his
message, the Prophet developed a sort of spiritual map, which
he drew on a deerskin. The map represented the path of the soul
from earth to heaven. According to the Prophet, the Great Spirit
had originally provided a special "avenue" for the Indians to
travel from earth to heaven. But the whites had blocked this
avenue. The Great Spirit had then opened another avenue for the
Indians, but it was much more difficult and dangerous than the
first.

A missionary who heard him preach reported that the Prophet
wept continuously as he spoke, holding the map in his hand and
pointing to the two avenues and the regions of heaven and earth.

Hear what the Great Spirit has ordered me to tell you! You are
to make sacrifices . . . to put off entirely from yourselves the
customs which you have adopted since the white people came
among us. You are to return to that former happy state, in which
we lived in peace and plenty, before these strangers came to
disturb us . . . Then will the Great Spirit give success to our arms;
then he will give us strength to conquer our enemies, to drive
them from hence, and recover the passage to the heavenly regions which they have taken from us.

The Delaware Prophet's message reached the ears of Pontiac,
a chief of the Ottawa tribe who lived near what is now Detroit,
Michigan. Although Pontiac was genuinely inspired by the
Prophet's message, he changed it to fit his own military and
political plans. The Delaware Prophet may have spoken against all

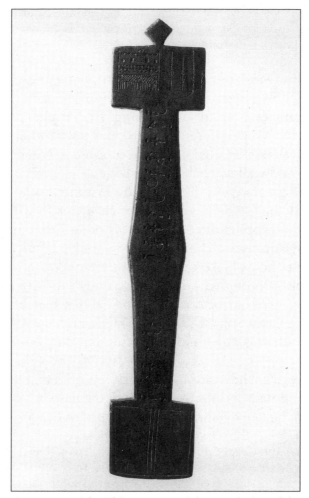

A prayer stick. This prayer stick was designed by Kenekuk, the Kickapoo Prophet (see profile on page 41). Kenekuk was influenced by the teachings of the Delaware Prophet, and his prayer stick is probably similar to those used by the earlier Prophet. (Catalogue No. 178369, Department of Anthropology, Smithsonian Institution)

whites, but Pontiac emphasized that the French were the Indians' brothers, who would help them against their English enemies. And while the Prophet prohibited the use of firearms, Pontiac said that the Indians should use guns to drive the British from the land.

In May 1763 the Indians of the Great Lakes region rose up against the British. Though often called Pontiac's Rebellion or Pontiac's War, it was really a united effort by many tribes under many leaders. During the first six weeks of fighting, the Indians captured eight British forts and forced the British to abandon a ninth fort.

Pontiac himself led the attack on Fort Detroit, one of the strongest British military outposts. The attack was originally planned as a surprise during a diplomatic visit, but the plan was betrayed and Pontiac's warriors were forced to retreat. They then began a six-month siege, with almost a thousand Indians ultimately surrounding the fort. The siege would have resulted in a great Indian victory had it not been for a group of British soldiers who brought supplies in late July.

In October, Pontiac received word that the war between the English and the French was officially over. The Treaty of Paris ending the war had actually been signed in February, but it took eight months for the news to reach Detroit. Knowing that their former French allies would no longer help the Indians, and facing a bleak winter without supplies, Pontiac gave up the siege on October 30 and retreated into what is now Illinois. Although some hostilities continued for two years, the strength of the rebellion was broken.

With the failure of the rebellion, the Delaware Prophet disappeared from the pages of recorded history. However, his message lived on, to be resurrected by other Indian prophets in other rebellions. The most famous of these were Tenskwatawa, the Shawnee Prophet, and Wovoka, the prophet of the Ghost Dance.

Although we do not even know his true name, the Delaware Prophet stands among the most important American Indian spiritual leaders. It was he who journeyed to the Master of Life and brought back the message of good living and a return to traditional Indian values. For the next 125 years, as the white invaders pushed the Indians farther and farther westward, the message of the Delaware Prophet moved westward as well, spreading like a religious wildfire across the continent.

HANDSOME LAKE

◆ ◆ ◆

Prophet of the Good Word

Before the Revolutionary War, the Iroquois Confederacy was the most organized and powerful tribal group north of Mexico. Centered in what is now upstate New York, the Iroquois originally included five tribes: the Mohawk, the Oneida, the Onondaga, the Cayuga, and the Seneca; a sixth tribe, the Tuscarora, joined the Confederacy in 1722. For almost a century the Iroquois played a shrewd diplomatic game between the French and British and controlled the rich fur trade with the tribes of the Ohio River Valley.

The great Iroquois Confederacy began to collapse during the American Revolution. Although they tried to remain neutral, four of the six tribes ultimately fought on the British side. In 1779, after a series of frontier attacks by Iroquois raiders, the American army marched through Iroquois territory and destroyed everything in its path. By the end of the war, only two out of 30 Iroquois towns remained undamaged.

The Americans treated the Iroquois like conquered enemies and forced them to give up most of their tribal lands. The Seneca—the largest and westernmost of the six tribes—held onto their land the longest. Finally, in 1797 the Seneca sold their land in the Treaty of Big Tree. They were allowed to keep 11 small reservations in what is now New York State. One Seneca chief, Cornplanter, also owned some private land on the Allegheny River in Pennsylvania, just south of the New York border.

Like most of the Iroquois, Cornplanter's Seneca were a frustrated, depressed people. Not only had they lost their land and their former power, but they had suffered through a series of harsh winters, devastating floods, and deadly epidemics of diseases brought by the whites. According to some estimates, the Iroquois population was cut in half during the 20-year period following the Revolutionary War.

Along with this loss of land, power, and population, there was great tension within families. Traditionally, Iroquois women owned the tribal land and raised the crops, while the men traveled as warriors, hunters, and diplomats. Now there was no need for warriors or diplomats, and the hunting grew worse every year. There was little for the men to do except hang around the village, getting drunk on cheap American whiskey. The women drank too, and many turned to witchcraft. Marriages fell apart. It was a bad time.

Cornplanter tried to help his people. The chief himself did not drink whiskey, and he encouraged others to be moderate in their habits. He also encouraged the Seneca to adopt some white ways, especially in farming and education. In 1798 three young Quakers came to live near Cornplanter's people and teach them how to farm with a plow and to raise livestock. They also offered instruction in reading and writing English and introduced Christian ideas to the Indians without trying to convert them. The arrival of the Quakers was a step toward a new way of living for Cornplanter's Seneca. But the most important force in the renewal of the Seneca was Cornplanter's older half-brother, Handsome Lake.

When the Quakers arrived, Handsome Lake was probably in his early sixties. He was originally from the village of Conawagas on the Genesee River in western New York. As a young man, he probably fought against the English in the French and Indian War and in Pontiac's Rebellion; he definitely fought against the Americans during the Revolutionary War. Now he shared Cornplanter's large double house in the village of Jenuchshadago, which means "Burnt House." Cornplanter and his family lived in one half of the house, while Handsome Lake lived in the other half with his daughter and grandchildren.

Like Cornplanter, Handsome Lake was one of 49 hereditary chiefs of the Iroquois Confederacy. He was also a respected herbalist—a medicine man who used the natural healing powers of plants. However, unlike his more moderate half-brother, Handsome Lake was very fond of the white man's whiskey.

In the winter of 1798–99, Handsome Lake went on a long hunting trip down the Allegheny River. That spring he and the other hunters canoed farther down the Allegheny to Pittsburgh, where they sold their furs and meat for various goods and supplies, including a large quantity of whiskey. By the time they returned to Burnt House, they were very drunk. The drinking continued for almost a month, with drunken men and women screaming, fighting, and stumbling through the village.

After this drinking binge, Handsome Lake became very ill, probably from too much alcohol and too little food. While he lay near death, Cornplanter and the Allegheny Seneca—with encouragement from the Quakers—took some steps toward reform. They decided to stop drinking whiskey and appointed two young chiefs to enforce the rule. They also decided to give up their wild dance parties—which they had learned from the whites—but to keep their traditional religious dances. Finally, they decided to crack down on witchcraft, and they put one alleged witch to death.

Although he was seriously ill, Handsome Lake knew of these changes, since the meetings were held next door in Cornplanter's house. On the morning of June 15, 1799, he stumbled out of bed and collapsed on the porch between the houses. Two hours later, he opened his eyes and described a great vision. In *The Death and Rebirth of the Seneca,* historian Anthony F. C. Wallace describes the beginning of the vision:

> Handsome Lake heard his name called and left the house. Outside he saw three middle-aged men dressed in fine ceremonial clothes with red paint on their faces and feathers in their bonnets, carrying bows and arrows in one hand and huckleberry bushes in the other. Handsome Lake collapsed from weakness, but the angels caught him and let him down gently. They told him they were sent by the Creator to visit Handsome Lake, whose constant thankfulness had earned him the right to help from his sickness.

The angels told Handsome Lake that the Strawberry Festival—a traditional Iroquois religious celebration—should be held every year, and that everyone should drink the strawberry juice. They also told him that there were four wicked sins that the Creator wanted to stop: the drinking of whiskey, the practice of witchcraft, the use of love potions, and the use of medicines that caused abortion or sterility. Minor sinners should confess their sins publicly; more serious sinners should confess to Handsome Lake; and the most serious sinners should confess directly to the Creator. Finally, the angels warned Handsome Lake never to drink again and promised that he would be visited by a fourth angel.

When he emerged from his vision, Handsome Lake was too exhausted to speak publicly. So Cornplanter called his people together and told them what his brother had seen. After the recent reforms, the vision of Handsome Lake had a powerful effect on the Seneca. Here was direct word from the Creator that they should continue on the path of reform. Henry Simmons, a Quaker who was present at the council, wrote: "I felt the love of God flowing powerfully amongst us."

After his first vision, Handsome Lake was still very ill. Almost two months later, on the night of August 7, he dreamed that the fourth angel appeared and offered to take him to the next world because he felt sorry for all his suffering. The following night Handsome Lake fell into a deep trance that lasted for seven hours. When he regained consciousness, he reported that he had been given a tour of the universe by a guide dressed in clear sky-blue clothing, carrying a bow and a single arrow.

The guide led Handsome Lake up into the sky along the Milky Way. As they ascended, he saw a series of images that represented various sins and problems—for example, a fat woman who represented the sin of gluttony; a church without a door or window that represented the Indians' problems with Christianity. About halfway to heaven they met George Washington, a good white man who had once told the Iroquois to live happily in their villages forever. Farther along the path they met Jesus, who asked Handsome Lake how his people accepted his (Handsome Lake's) teachings. When Handsome Lake replied that about half the people believed him, Jesus said, "You are more successful than I, for some believe in you but none in me."

The guide then showed Handsome Lake a fork in the sky path, where a narrow road led to heaven and a wide road led to hell. Handsome Lake noticed that more children than adults went to heaven, but the guide told him that all people receive three chances to repent their sins and accept the *Gaiwiio*, which means the "Good Word." The guide led Handsome Lake down the wide path to the realm of punishment—a great iron lodge of fire and hot wind. There the Punisher created cruel punishments that fit the crime. A man who beat his wife was forced to beat a red-hot image of a woman. A couple who fought were forced to quarrel until their eyes and tongues bulged out of their heads.

After this vision of hell, the guide took Handsome Lake on the narrow road to heaven. There he met his own son, who had been dead for several years, and Cornplanter's daughter, who had been dead for seven months. Both of these dead children expressed concern that their living brothers were not showing proper respect for their fathers.

The spirit guide showed Handsome Lake many canoes loaded with whiskey, and emphasized that he must stay away from liquor. He said that it was good for white people to teach Seneca children—as long as the Seneca agreed to it—but that it was good to keep some of their traditional ways, too. Finally, he warned that a great sickness would strike the village if the Seneca did not improve their behavior and that "his people must collect together in worship, and cook a white dog and every one eat thereof, as a preventative against the sickness."

When he regained consciousness, Handsome Lake told Cornplanter all that he had seen. The White Dog Feast, a traditional Iroquois ceremony, was held the next day. When the Quaker Henry Simmons visited Handsome Lake the day after the feast, he found that the sickly old man had regained his health.

Six months later, on February 5, 1800, Handsome Lake had a third vision, in which the angels told him that the whites were wrong to take all the Indian lands and to insist that their book (the Bible) contained all the truth. They ordered Handsome Lake to create a book of his own, so that the Indians might always remember his teachings and the children would be raised in the Gaiwiio, the Good Word. They said that Cornplanter should visit all the Iroquois towns and try to unify the people. They also emphasized that the Iroquois must keep their old forms of worship, especially the Midwinter Ceremony.

These three visions formed the basis of Handsome Lake's teachings. He did not really consider the teachings to be a new religion; rather he saw them as a return to the traditional religion of the Iroquois. However, Handsome Lake's teachings combined Christian and Iroquois ideas. The Iroquois had a creation myth of two twins, one good and the other evil. Now this struggle between good and evil was seen as a Christian-type struggle between the Great Spirit and the Punisher. The idea of hell is also a Christian concept, as is the idea of recording all the teachings in a single book.

By the time of his third vision, Handsome Lake had achieved religious power among the Allegheny Seneca. In the fall of 1800, he entered a struggle for control of the entire Seneca Nation. The

Handsome Lake preaching in a longhouse while holding a wampum belt. Drawn around 1905 by Jesse Cornplanter, a Seneca artist descended from Handsome Lake's half-brother, Cornplanter. (Courtesy of the New York State Library, Manuscripts and Special Collections)

conflict began with the illness of Cornplanter's daughter. Handsome Lake decided that the young woman had been bewitched by some visiting Delaware Indians. Other Seneca leaders questioned Handsome Lake's vision and spiritual authority, particularly when the conflict threatened to explode into a war between the Seneca and the Delaware. Handsome Lake then widened his accusations of witchcraft to include those Seneca who opposed him. Among the accused was Red Jacket, Handsome Lake's nephew and the official speaker for the Seneca Nation.

A great council was called to discuss the question of witchcraft. The council approved Handsome Lake's position against witchcraft but found Red Jacket not guilty. The council also voted to forbid whiskey among the Seneca and to appoint Handsome Lake as "High Priest and principal Sachem, in all things Civil and Religious." In effect, this made Handsome Lake the religious dictator of the Seneca Nation.

With his new power, Handsome Lake continued to attack witchcraft among the Seneca. It is unclear how many accused witches were actually put to death during this witch hunt. However, most of those accused probably saved their lives by repenting and confessing to Handsome Lake.

Handsome Lake's witch hunt was not popular with many of the Seneca, and his opposition to "progress" caused additional dissent. Although the spirit guide in his second vision had said that it was all right for the whites to teach Indian children—if the Seneca could all agree on it—Handsome Lake took a strong stand against white education. He also was against selling land or selling crops.

This put him in direct conflict with Cornplanter, who believed that education and modern farming methods would help the Seneca improve their lives. After a period of conflict, Handsome Lake changed his position and admitted that "the white people were going to settle all around them [and] that they could not live unless they learned to farm, and followed the white people's ways . . ."

This change in attitude actually increased Handsome Lake's power and popularity. In 1801 he was elected to the Seneca tribal

council. The following year, in March 1802, he led a Seneca delegation that met President Thomas Jefferson in Washington, D.C.
The main purpose of the visit was to establish Seneca land claims
and discuss plans for government aid to help modernize their
farming methods.

Handsome Lake told Jefferson of his visions of the four angels
and said that he had been appointed as a fifth angel to bring the
message of the Great Spirit to the earth. President Jefferson replied
that it would be good for all the Indians to follow the teachings of
Handsome Lake. He gave the Seneca farming equipment, promised to establish their land claims in writing, and said that Congress was considering a law forbidding Indians to drink alcohol.

Later, Jefferson wrote a long letter to Handsome Lake in which
he gave his "stamp of approval" to the Prophet's new religion:

> Go on, then, brother, in the great reformation you have undertaken.
> Persuade our red man to be sober and to cultivate their lands;
> and their women to spin and weave for their families . . . It will
> be a great glory to you to have been the instrument of so happy
> a change, and your children's children, from generation to gen-
> eration, will repeat your name with love and gratitude forever.

Around this time, Handsome Lake began to add social ideas
to his religious teachings. Some of these ideas were influenced
by the Quakers, who taught by example rather than by lecturing
about Christianity and white culture. The Seneca could see the
Quakers' model farm, their hard work, their healthy family
lives, and their good habits.

In traditional Iroquois society, the relationship between a
mother and her daughter was stronger than the relationship
between a woman and her husband. The land was passed down
from mother to daughter, and the men were usually away from
home—hunting, making war, or conducting diplomacy. Divorce
was easy, and mothers often encouraged their daughters to take
up with another man.

The new Iroquois economy—which was based on the white
model of a family farm—required a stronger relationship between the husband and wife. In order for a family farm to be

successful, the family must stay together. Handsome Lake taught that divorce was a sin, and that the husband and wife must not quarrel. Parents must treat their children kindly, and children must respect their parents. He also emphasized that the wife's mother should not interfere with her daughter's family life.

Among Handsome Lake's other social teachings was the idea that the whites were not bad people; they were just different from the Indians. He believed that Jesus was the true Messiah of the whites, while he—Handsome Lake—was the true Messiah of the Indians. Although he had originally been against white-style education, he now believed that education was good for the Indians as long as they did not give up their traditional religious practices.

Handsome Lake's teachings passed quickly from the Seneca to the other Iroquois nations. In 1803 the great Council Fire of the Iroquois Confederacy was moved to the village of Burnt House in recognition of Handsome Lake's authority. However, many Iroquois refused to accept Handsome Lake as supreme leader of the Six Nations. Ironically, the movement of the Council Fire—which should have been his greatest moment—was the beginning of Handsome Lake's downfall.

A short time later, Handsome Lake quarreled with Cornplanter and moved with his followers to Cold Spring, up the Allegheny River in New York. There the Quakers resisted his plans to build a traditional Indian village, which they considered a step backward in Seneca "progress." Around the same time, Handsome Lake was attacked as a false prophet by Red Jacket, and the Council Fire was moved back to Red Jacket's village of Buffalo Creek in 1807. That year Handsome Lake began another series of witch hunts that resulted in several brutal murders of alleged witches.

Although his political power declined, Handsome Lake's religious ideas continued to spread, not only among the Iroquois, but among the western Indians of the Ohio River Valley. While Indians who converted to Christianity often struggled with their new beliefs, the converts to Handsome Lake's religion seemed very happy—perhaps because they were living a good life while keeping the best of their old customs. They were also prosperous because of his emphasis on hard work and the family farm.

When the War of 1812 broke out, Handsome Lake encouraged the Indians to stay out of the fighting. He became known as the "Peace Prophet," as opposed to Tenskwatawa, the Shawnee religious leader who was called the "War Prophet." Ironically, Tenskwatawa was originally inspired by the visions and teachings of Handsome Lake. Although many Iroquois did fight on the American side in the war, Handsome Lake's peace message was obeyed by most of his followers.

On August 10, 1815, Handsome Lake died while visiting the Onondaga Reservation. An obituary in a Buffalo newspaper said he was 66 years old, but he was probably closer to 80. During the years after his death, the Iroquois faced pressure from a new wave of Christian missionaries who—unlike the Quakers—insisted that the Indians give up their traditional religion and convert to Christianity. In response to this pressure, the Iroquois divided into two groups: Christian and "pagan."

Beginning around 1818, the "pagan" Iroquois developed the story of Handsome Lake's life and teachings into a collection called the *Code of Handsome Lake*. There are different versions of the Code, depending upon the preacher, but the most popular version was created by Handsome Lake's grandson, Jimmy Johnson, who preached at the village of Tonawanda in the 1840s.

A new organized religion grew along with the Code. This religion became known as the Longhouse Religion, named after the traditional Iroquois building in which the religious meetings are held. The Longhouse Religion is still practiced by many Iroquois today. Although it contains some Christian ideas, especially of the Quakers, it is a uniquely Indian religion based on the Gaiwiio—the Good Word of Handsome Lake.

TENSKWATAWA

◆ ◆ ◆

The Shawnee Prophet

After the Revolutionary War, American settlers streamed across the Appalachian Mountains to carve farms and towns out of the wilderness. The first settlements were in Kentucky and Tennessee, but land-hungry settlers soon pushed across the Ohio River into what is now southern Ohio. According to an earlier treaty, the Ohio River was supposed to be the boundary line between the whites and the Indians. Faced with this trespassing on their lands, the tribes of the Ohio River Valley resisted the whites in a series of bloody battles that ended with Indian defeat at the Battle of Fallen Timbers in 1794.

The following year a new treaty was signed at Fort Greenville in western Ohio. The Treaty of Greenville moved the old boundary line between the races, opening most of present-day Ohio to white settlement. Within a few years over 40,000 Americans poured into the Ohio country, and Ohio became a state in 1803. However, this rapid settlement simply increased the desire for Indian land. At the same time, many Indians refused to move out of the Ohio country.

Among those who refused to move was a Shawnee leader named Tecumseh. The Shawnee were one of the most powerful tribes in the Ohio Valley region. They had been pushed from homelands in Pennsylvania and Kentucky by earlier white settlers; now they were determined to make a stand, and Tecumseh was destined to lead the last great Indian rebellion in the Ohio Valley region. But the man who inspired the rebellion was his younger brother, Tenskwatawa, the Shawnee Prophet.

Tenskwatawa was born in 1775, one of a set of triplets. Tecumseh was seven years older, born in 1768. Both were from the village of Piqua, on the Mad River near present-day Springfield, Ohio. Their father was a Shawnee chief who died fighting white settlers in 1774, before the birth of the triplets. Their mother was a Creek woman who left her children a few years later to join her own people in the South.

Thus Tenskwatawa never knew his father and barely knew his mother, while Tecumseh knew them only in childhood. The brothers were raised by family members, including two older brothers and an older sister. Like their father, the older brothers both died in battles with the whites. It is not surprising that Tecumseh later said that the sight of a white man made his skin crawl.

While Tecumseh developed into a respected warrior and hunter, Tenskwatawa was an unhappy and troubled youth. His childhood name, Lalawethika, means "the Rattle" or "Noise-maker," apparently a description of his loud boasting. As a child he put out his right eye playing with a bow and arrow, and he began to drink heavily as a teenager. While his older brother was emerging as a tribal leader, Tenskwatawa was heading for a life of drunken misery.

During the spring of 1805, when he was 30 years old, Tenskwatawa experienced a religious conversion that changed his life and the life of his people. While reaching into a fire to light his pipe, he collapsed on the ground unconscious—his eyes closed, with no sign of breathing. Thinking he was dead, his wife began to make arrangements for his funeral. But before the arrangements were completed, Tenskwatawa regained consciousness and reported that he had been taken on a journey by two spirit guides sent from the Master of Life.

First the guides showed him paradise—a beautiful hunting ground with abundant game, fish, and cornfields. This was what awaited those Indians who lived a good life. Then he saw the devil and the fiery punishment that awaited those Indians who followed the path of sin. Tenskwatawa vowed to lead a good life and give up drinking and other sins. He would no longer be called Lalawethika, "the Rattle." He was now Tenskwatawa, "the Open Door," because he would show his people an open door to a new and better way of life.

During the following months, Tenskwatawa experienced more visions and further developed his teachings. Although many Shawnee were skeptical that the loud, drunken braggart had really become a holy man, others gathered around him as a prophet who would help them improve their lives. That summer he moved with his followers to a new village near Greenville, Ohio.

In November 1805, Tenskwatawa announced to the neighboring tribes that he was now a prophet in direct communication with the Master of Life. He said that drunkenness, witchcraft, and intermarriage between Indian women and white men were terrible sins. The Master of Life wanted the Indians to share all property in common and to give up all white ways and products, including guns, clothing, and the flint and steel they used to make fires.

From then on, hunting must be with a bow and arrow, clothing must be made from animal skins, and fires must be started by rubbing two sticks together. A fire must burn continually in every lodge, for when the fire went out, so did the life of the Indians. Children must respect their parents, and the young must care for the old. Finally, the Prophet claimed that he had received power from the Great Spirit to cure sickness, confuse their enemies, and overcome the power of death.

The teachings of Tenskwatawa were clearly influenced by earlier spiritual leaders, especially the Delaware Prophet, who had preached in the Ohio Valley 40 years earlier, and Handsome Lake, the Seneca prophet who had experienced a similar tour of the universe in 1799. Other influences included the white Shakers, whose services Tenskwatawa attended, and an old Shawnee medicine man named Penagashea, who died shortly before Tenskwatawa announced his vision. But Tenskwatawa had a personal charisma that gave his teachings a new power.

Although he claimed to be the Open Door, the first result of the Prophet's teachings was a closed door for those he accused of witchcraft. Among the earliest victims were several Delaware

Indians, who were tortured and killed by their own tribe in the winter of 1805–06. The deaths of the accused Delaware witches brought a written response from William Henry Harrison, governor of the Indiana Territory. Harrison asked the Delaware to question the new prophet before carrying out his orders:

> Demand of him some proofs at least, of his being the messenger of the Deity . . . If he is really a prophet, ask of him to cause the sun to stand still—the moon to alter its course—the rivers to cease to flow—or the dead to raise from their graves. If he does these things, you may believe that he has been sent from God.

Harrison's letter created new doubts about Tenskwatawa's power. Then in the summer of 1806, the Shawnee Prophet provided the exact proof that Harrison had requested. Tenskwatawa told the unbelievers that he would demonstrate his supernatural powers by bringing darkness over the face of the sun. In fact he correctly predicted that a solar eclipse would occur on June 16. During the eclipse he stood in the midday darkness and shouted, "Did I not speak truth? See, the sun is dark!"

This success greatly increased the Prophet's power and prestige. Word of his teachings spread across the Indian lands from Florida to Saskatchewan. John Tanner, a white captive who lived among the Ojibwa in what is now northern Minnesota, reported a visit from the Prophet's messengers and a special ceremony by which the new converts accepted the Prophet's teachings:

> Four strings of mouldy and discoloured beans . . . which we were told were made of the flesh itself of the prophet, were carried with much solemnity to each man in the lodge, and he was expected to take hold of each string at the top, and draw them gently through his hand. This was called shaking hands with the prophet, and was considered as solemnly engaging to obey his injunctions, and accept his mission as from the Supreme.

In the spring of 1807, the U.S. government agent at Fort Wayne, Indiana, estimated that 1,500 Indians passed his post on their way to the Prophet's village at Greenville. Alarmed by this growing movement, the agent demanded that the Indians retreat beyond the dividing line set by the Treaty of Greenville. The Prophet's older brother Tecumseh rejected the government demand in clear, "fighting" words:

> These lands are ours. No one has a right to remove us, because we were the first owners. The Great Spirit above has appointed this place for us, on which to light our fires, and here we will remain. As to boundaries, the Great Spirit above knows no boundaries nor will his red children acknowledge any.

Tecumseh's speech marked a new direction in the Indian movement. When the Shawnee Prophet first announced his mission from the Master of Life, the emphasis of his teachings was a return to traditional Indian values and spirituality. Now Tecumseh was suggesting a new emphasis—a political and military resistance to white settlement in the Ohio Valley. However, it would take several years before Tecumseh's message would take root among the tribes. In the meantime Tenskwatawa was still the leader of the Indians at Greenville.

Although ready to fulfill the spiritual needs of his followers, the Prophet found it difficult to feed so many people gathered in one place. The fields around the village were small, and the hunting was poor. To make matters worse, there were too many white settlements and unfriendly Indian villages in the area. The Prophet's most devoted followers were further west, among the tribes of Michigan, Illinois, and Wisconsin.

In the spring of 1808, Tenskwatawa and Tecumseh moved to a new village at the junction of the Wabash and Tippecanoe rivers in what is now western Indiana. This village was originally named Kehtipaquononk, which means "the great clearing," but the whites pronounced it "Tippecanoe." Now it became known as Prophetstown.

During the next three years, Prophetstown became the center of antiwhite activity on the frontier. At first the Indians were drawn by the spiritual teachings of Tenskwatawa, and the white authorities naturally believed that Tenskwatawa was the leader of the Indian resistance movement. But it soon became apparent that the real force at Prophetstown was Tecumseh.

Tenskwatawa, the Shawnee Prophet. From a drawing by Pierre Le Dru, a young French trader who sketched the Prophet at Vincennes, Indiana, in 1808, shortly after Tenskwatawa moved to Prophetstown. (National Anthropological Archives, Smithsonian Institution)

Tenskwatawa was an intelligent, charismatic man and a strong public speaker. But he was not a dynamic military leader who could rally the tribes behind him. Tecumseh was such a man. He was a brave war chief, a great hunter, and a brilliant speaker. He had a dignity, fairness, and strength of character that impressed all those who met him—white or Indian. William Henry Harrison, who battled Tecumseh for many years, called him "one of those uncommon geniuses which spring up occasionally to produce revolutions and overturn the established order of things."

Revolution was exactly what Tecumseh had in mind. He dreamed of uniting the Indian tribes in a great confederacy to drive the whites south of the Ohio River. He envisioned an Indian utopia, where all the tribes would share the land in common. Tenskwatawa's teachings of a return to traditional Indian values and shared property fit perfectly with Tecumseh's plans.

Tenskwatawa was a proud man, but he recognized his older brother's leadership and supported the great confederacy. While the Prophet remained the spiritual leader of Prophetstown, Tecumseh traveled among the tribes, preaching Indian unity and war against the Americans. British authorities in Canada—who were preparing for the War of 1812—encouraged Tecumseh's efforts and gave him guns, ammunition, and other supplies.

In 1809 Governor Harrison tricked a group of drunken "chiefs" into signing away three million acres of land in what is now Indiana and Illinois for $5,000 worth of supplies and a small increase in their annual government payments. This unfair land sale inflamed antiwhite feelings among the Ohio Valley Indians. Many who were originally drawn by the Prophet's spiritual ideas now turned wholeheartedly to Tecumseh's military plans.

Although Tecumseh confronted Governor Harrison about the treaty, he kept his angry warriors under control. Tecumseh had studied earlier Indian rebellions; he knew that timing and unity were essential to success. He would not attack until the time was right and the Indians were united.

In the summer of 1811, Tecumseh left Prophetstown to enlist support from the tribes of the South. He and Tenskwatawa agreed that the Prophet would not be drawn into battle while he was gone. However, Governor Harrison decided to take advantage of Tecumseh's absence to destroy the Indian confederacy. On November 5, 1811, he marched toward Prophetstown with over 1,000 men.

The following day, as Harrison approached the Indian village, he was met by messengers from Tenskwatawa, who said that the

Prophet did not want to fight. Harrison agreed to a truce and promised to meet with Tenskwatawa the next day. However, as a precaution, he ordered his troops to sleep on their weapons, ready for battle. It was a wise move.

That night Tenskwatawa told his warriors that he had used his supernatural powers to kill half the soldiers and drive the other half crazy. All the Indians would have to do, he said, was march into the camp and finish them off with their hatchets. No one knows exactly why Tenskwatawa decided to attack Harrison against Tecumseh's orders, but around the time Tecumseh left for the South, the British contacted the Prophet and told him it was time to take up the hatchet against the Americans. Tenskwatawa may have resented Tecumseh's power and wanted to regain his old authority. And the younger, hotheaded warriors probably pushed him into the conflict.

A little after four in the morning of November 7, about 700 Indian warriors attacked Harrison's camp outside Prophetstown. Because of Harrison's order to sleep on their weapons, the U.S. soldiers were able to respond quickly and defend themselves against the initial surprise attack. While the warriors fought in bloody hand-to-hand combat, the Prophet stood on a hillside, praying and working his medicine. But his supernatural powers could not stop the soldiers. The battle raged until daylight, when a final charge by the U.S. troops drove the Indians back into a swamp, where they scattered into the wilderness.

Governor Harrison claimed the Battle of Tippecanoe as a great victory, but losses were heavy on both sides. At least 62 whites were killed and another 126 were wounded, while the Indians lost around 50 dead and 75 wounded. Despite their losses, the whites achieved their purpose. The following day Harrison's army found Prophetstown deserted and burned it to the ground.

The destruction of Prophetstown marked the end of Tecumseh's great confederacy and the end of Tenskwatawa's power. The surviving warriors were so angry with their former Prophet that they tied him up and threatened to kill him. "You are a liar," cried a Winnebago warrior, "for you told us that the white people were dead or crazy, when they were all in their senses and fought like the devil."

When Tecumseh returned from the South, he too was furious at Tenskwatawa for launching the attack. According to some sources, Tecumseh grabbed the Prophet by the hair and shook him violently, calling him a child and threatening to kill him if he ever did anything again to weaken the great Indian confederacy. While the Prophet nursed his bruised ego, Tecumseh tried to put the confederacy back together.

In the summer of 1812, Tecumseh went to Fort Malden, Canada to obtain guns and ammunition from the British. Shortly after he arrived, word reached the fort that Great Britain and the United States were officially at war. Tecumseh stayed in Canada to fight for the British and was commissioned as a brigadier general in the British army.

With Tecumseh away in Canada, Tenskwatawa attempted to reestablish his power on the American frontier. He moved back to the site of Prophetstown and gathered several hundred warriors around him. But he no longer had the spiritual authority he held before the Battle of Tippecanoe. After an unsuccessful attack against the Americans at Fort Harrison, the warriors began to drift away from Prophetstown. In December 1812, Tenskwatawa fled to Canada and joined Tecumseh.

Although he was present at several battles during the War of 1812, Tenskwatawa never participated in the fighting. He was a holy man, not a warrior. Just as he had done at the Battle of Tippecanoe, he stood back from the fighting, praying and making medicine for the warriors' success. Tecumseh, on the other hand, fought bravely until he was killed in the Battle of the Thames on October 5, 1813. Despite his high rank, he died in hand-to-hand combat, dressed as a common warrior.

After Tecumseh's death, the Prophet claimed to be the "principal chief of all the Western Nations." In fact, his power was now based on his ability to obtain food and supplies from the British for his followers. In the glorious days of Prophetstown, he and Tecumseh had denounced the "government chiefs" who depended on the Americans for power. Now Tenskwatawa himself was a government chief for the British.

When the war ended in 1815, William Henry Harrison invited Tenskwatawa to return to the United States as a common Indian but not as a chief. The Prophet refused this offer and stayed in Canada, where he lived on rations from the British government. Some of his followers resettled in villages near Prophetstown, hoping that the Prophet would return and the great Indian resistance movement would begin again. But the Prophet did not return. The resistance movement in the Ohio River Valley was over.

During his exile in Canada, Tenskwatawa became frustrated as the rations from the British government grew smaller and smaller with each passing year. He was also frustrated with his own loss of power. Finally, in 1824, the American government made him an offer he couldn't refuse. The Americans wanted to force the Shawnee to move from their homeland in Ohio and settle west of the Mississippi River. They needed a Shawnee leader who would help them convince the other Shawnee to leave. And Tenskwatawa, the Shawnee Prophet, was just the man for the job.

In *The Shawnee Prophet*, historian R. David Edmunds suggests several reasons why Tenskwatawa—a man who once led the fight to hold onto Indian lands—now agreed to act as a spokesman for Indian removal:

> Not only could he return to the United States, but . . . he would again attain some status as a leader, even if only as a government chief. In addition, the move west would bring him closer to the Sacs, Foxes, and Kickapoos, tribes over whom he once had exercised great influence. Finally, the government's rationale for the removal, that the Indians would be given an abundant new land in the west, far from the corrupting influence of evil white men, must have held some attraction for him. He no longer claimed to be a prophet, but a homeland free of whites, where Indians could practice their traditional way of life, had once formed the basis for his religious movement.

In 1825, Tenskwatawa arrived in Ohio and began to develop support for the removal. He met with resistance at first, but by the following year he had convinced about 250 Shawnee to move with him west of the Mississippi. The group left in September 1826, but the journey proved harder and longer than anyone had imagined. In May 1828, after almost two years on the trail, the Shawnee finally reached their reservation in Kansas.

Tenskwatawa died in November 1836 in what is now Kansas City, Kansas. In 1832, four years before his death, he was visited by the American painter George Catlin. Catlin painted his portrait and talked with him about the glorious days of the great confederacy. Catlin's report of this meeting provides insight into Tenskwatawa's character, at least in his old age:

> This, no doubt, has been a very shrewd and influential man, but circumstances have destroyed him, as they have many other great men before him, and he now lives respected, but silent and melancholy, in his tribe. I conversed with him a great deal about his brother Tecumseh, of whom he spoke frankly, and seemingly with great pleasure; but of himself and his own great schemes he would say nothing. He told me that Tecumseh's plans were to embody all the Indian tribes in a grand confederacy . . . to unite their forces in an army that would be able to meet and drive back the white people, who were continually advancing on the Indian tribes and forcing them from their lands toward the Rocky Mountains; that Tecumseh was a great general, and that nothing but his premature death defeated his grand plan.

It is interesting that Tenskwatawa, whom many whites considered to be an egotistical, loudmouthed fraud, refused to speak of his own accomplishments but rather spoke only of his brother. And yet, Tecumseh's great vision of Indian unity really began with the spiritual vision of Tenskwatawa, the Shawnee Prophet.

KENEKUK

◆ ◆ ◆

The Kickapoo Prophet

In the early days of our country, the Kickapoo were the strongest tribe in what is now Indiana and Illinois. Although united by language and customs, the Kickapoo developed into two different groups that were separated by geography. One group, called the Vermilion Kickapoo, lived near the Wabash and Vermilion rivers on either side of the Illinois-Indiana border. The other group, called the Prairie Kickapoo, settled further west on the prairies of central and western Illinois.

The Kickapoo violently resisted the white intruders who moved westward after the Revolutionary War. However, around 1795—after a series of defeats by the Americans—the Vermillion Kickapoo decided to stay on their land and try to live peacefully with their new American neighbors. The Prairie Kickapoo remained hostile to the Americans and moved farther away from white settlements.

After the War of 1812 (1812–15) a great wave of white settlers poured into Illinois and Indiana. To make room for the whites, U.S. government agents tried to convince the Indians who lived in the area to move west of the Mississippi River. It didn't matter whether they were peaceful or hostile—they all had to go.

In the face of this pressure, a brilliant young leader emerged among the peaceful Vermilion Kickapoo. His name was Kenekuk. Some scholars have translated his name as "putting his foot down." This is an appropriate meaning, because Kenekuk devoted his life to keeping tribal land and customs in the face of white settlement.

Kenekuk was born around 1790. According to Kickapoo tradition, he was a wild young man who killed his uncle in a drunken rage. Expelled from the tribe, he went to live on the outskirts of the white settlements, where he was taken in by a Catholic priest. One day the priest discovered him looking through some books in his library. The young Kickapoo explained that he wanted to know what was in the books, so the priest began to teach him about Christianity. Kenekuk learned quickly, and the priest told him that if he brought these teachings back to his own people he would be forgiven for the murder of his uncle.

We don't know if this story is true, but Kenekuk did preach a new religion that combined Christian ideas with traditional Indian concepts. His followers believed in heaven and hell, confessed their sins, and held Sunday services. At the same time, they sang their traditional Kickapoo songs, refused to learn English, and interpreted the Christian practices in uniquely Indian ways.

The Kickapoo Prophet claimed that he gained his religious knowledge directly from the Great Spirit, who gave Kenekuk a piece of His heart and sent him to teach the Indians the right path. Kenekuk explained, "I have had the good fortune to be instructed by the Great Spirit in a good and correct course." Although Kenekuk spoke of Jesus as a great prophet who died for the sins of the whites, he claimed that he—Kenekuk—was the prophet who had come to save the Indians.

Like the Delaware Prophet and the Shawnee Prophet before him, Kenekuk told his followers to live peacefully with each other, to stay away from alcohol, and to give up the medicine song and the medicine bag, which he considered superstitions. He encouraged the Kickapoo warriors to stop painting their bodies, to give up the warpath, and to take up farming, which was traditionally considered woman's work.

Like the earlier prophets, Kenekuk created a prayer stick for his people. Carved from maple wood, the prayer stick had a representation of heaven at the top and hell at the bottom. In between were 15 Kickapoo symbols, arranged in three groups of five. Using it in a manner similar to a Catholic rosary, Kenekuk's followers ran their fingers along the stick, pausing at each symbol to recite a prayer. (A photograph of Kennekuk's prayer stick appears on page 18.)

Kenekuk developed a diagram of the path from earth to heaven that was similar to the Delaware Prophet's map of the soul. According to Kenekuk's diagram, the Indians had reached a turning point in their spiritual development. At this point, "the Great Spirit gave his blessings to the Indians and told them . . . to throw away their medicine bags, and not to steal, not to tell lies, not to quarrel . . ." Only by following these rules could the Indians take the straight path that would lead to heaven.

Although influenced by the Delaware and Shawnee Prophets, Kenekuk was much more than an imitator. Whereas the older prophets saw Indian spiritual renewal as the first step toward driving the whites from the land, Kenekuk believed that the Indians and whites must live together in peace. "Every red and white man is my brother," he said, "and I desire to be united with them in [friendship], and for this reason I am afraid of nothing."

In 1819 some Kickapoo leaders signed two treaties giving up their lands in Indiana and Illinois in exchange for land in Missouri. During the next few years, around 2,000 Kickapoo crossed the Mississippi River. The Kickapoo were unhappy with their new homeland, and many moved on to Oklahoma, Texas, and Mexico.

After the great Kickapoo migration, two major bands remained in Illinois. One was the Vermilion Kickapoo, led by Kenekuk. The other was a band of Prairie Kickapoo led by Mecina. Neither Kenekuk nor Mecina had signed the treaties of 1819. They agreed that no man—red or white—could own or sell the land, that all the land belonged to the Great Spirit. But though Kenekuk and Mecina shared the same goal—to hold on to their land in the face of white settlement—they took different approaches to achieving this goal.

Some white historians have portrayed Mecina as a fierce chief whose warriors terrorized the Illinois country. Actually, the violence of Mecina's warriors was exaggerated by the white settlers of Illinois because they wanted the U.S. government to remove the Indians. And the settlers themselves started many violent conflicts. However, it is true that Mecina and his warriors threatened the settlers with violence if they tried to remove them from their beloved land.

Kenekuk made no threats. He did not believe in violence. Instead he practiced a nonviolent form of resistance, similar to that of 20th-century spiritual leaders like Gandhi and Martin Luther King, Jr. Kenekuk's people simply stayed on their farms in Illinois, living peacefully among themselves and with their white neighbors. In order to buy time, Kenekuk played a long diplomatic game with William Clark, the superintendent of Indian affairs for the region.

William Clark is famous as the co-leader of the Lewis and Clark expedition, which traveled to the Pacific Northwest in 1804–06. However, Clark was also one of the fairest Indian agents to serve the U.S. government. During the 1820s he sent messengers to Kenekuk, asking when he planned to leave. The Kickapoo Prophet listened politely and assured the messengers that he would leave when the time was right, but of course the time was never right. Perhaps the corn was not ready, or there was sickness among his band, or the Great Spirit had simply told him to wait.

At least once a year, Kenekuk visited Clark in St. Louis and made long, passionate speeches explaining his position. In 1827 Clark sent a written translation of one of Kenekuk's speeches to his superiors in Washington, D.C. This speech provides us with a fascinating glimpse of Kenekuk's thinking and personality:

> My father, the Great Spirit has placed us all on this earth; he has given to our nation a piece of land. Why do you want to take it away and give us so much trouble? We ought to live in peace and happiness among ourselves and with you . . . My father, you call the redskins your children. When we have children, we treat them well. That is the reason I make this long talk and get you to take pity on us and let us remain where we are.

Still speaking to Clark, Kenekuk directed his remarks to the president of the United States, whom he called the Great Father:

> My Great Father . . . I want to talk to you mildly and in peace, so that we may understand each other. When I saw the Great Spirit, he told me to throw all our bad acts away. We did so. Some of our chiefs said the land belonged to us, the Kickapoos; but this is not

Kenekuk, the Kickapoo Prophet. From a painting by George Catlin, entitled The Foremost Man, Chief of the Tribe, *painted in 1831 near Danville, Illinois. Catlin described Kenekuk as "a very shrewd and talented man."* (National Museum of American Art, Smithsonian Institution, Gift of Mrs. Joseph Harrison, Jr.)

what the Great Spirit told me—the lands belong to him . . . When I saw the Great Spirit, he told me, Mention all this to your Great Father. He will take pity on your situation and let you remain on the lands where you are for some years, and [then] you will get to a clear piece of land where you will all be happy.

Kenekuk finished his speech with a flourish that marks him as one of the great orators of the 19th century:

> My father, we are sitting by each other to tell the truth. If you write anything wrong, the Great Spirit will know it. If I say anything not true, the Great Spirit will hear it . . . My father, everything belongs to the Great Spirit. If he chooses to make the earth shake, or turn it over, all the skins, white and red, can not stop it. I have done. I trust to the Great Spirit.

Clark was patient with Kenekuk's speeches and excuses because the Vermilion Kickapoo lived peacefully and threatened no one. During the presidency of John Quincy Adams, the U.S. government was also patient. However, the whites of Illinois pressured the federal government to remove the Indians, and when Andrew Jackson became president in 1829 the federal policy changed dramatically. All Indians, whether peaceful or not, would be removed west of the Mississippi.

The last violent resistance in the Illinois region was the Black Hawk War, led by a leader of the Sauk and Fox who lived in northwestern Illinois. In the spring and summer of 1832, Black Hawk and his warriors—including some Prairie Kickapoo—fought a series of bloody battles with U.S. and Illinois forces that ended in defeat for the Indians.

True to his philosophy of peace, Kenekuk and the Vermilion Kickapoo stayed out of the Black Hawk War. Although some of Mecina's warriors fought with Black Hawk, Mecina himself joined Kenekuk's peaceful band. But the time for peaceful negotiation had passed. After the Black Hawk War, government pressure increased and Kenekuk finally agreed to move his people west of the Mississippi.

In the fall of 1832, Kenekuk and other Kickapoo leaders signed a treaty trading their lands in Illinois and Missouri for a smaller homeland in northeastern Kansas. Kenekuk left the Vermilion River with around 400 people, including over 100 Potawatomi who had converted to his religion. After camping for the winter east of the Mississippi, they continued on to Kansas in the spring. There they settled along the Missouri River north of Fort Leavenworth.

A mile away, the Prairie Kickapoo lived in their own village. They looked down upon Kenekuk's band and called the warriors "squaws." However, Kenekuk's people continued to follow the path of nonviolence, living in peace and working the land. The Kansas soil was fertile, and there was enough water and timber for their needs. The Kickapoo's greatest concern was that the U.S. government did not give them the money and supplies promised in the Treaty of 1832. But even without the government's help, the Vermilion Kickapoo made a good life in their new homeland.

During the next 10 years, a long parade of Christian missionaries attempted to save the "pagan" souls of Kenekuk's followers. The missionaries believed that they would gain many converts among Kenekuk's people, because their religion seemed to be similar to Christianity—at least on the outside. However, they discovered that Kenekuk's people were devoted to their Prophet and happy with their own religion.

Kenekuk played a diplomatic game with these missionaries similar to his diplomacy with William Clark. He knew that the missionaries could help his people receive the money and supplies they had been promised by the government, so he assured them that the Kickapoo were good Christians. He even allowed a Methodist missionary to baptize himself and his followers. But the ceremonies of the white missionaries were not important to Kenekuk and his people. They had their own ceremonies.

According to the missionaries, Kenekuk held two services during the week. On Friday night, after a speech by the Prophet, his followers confessed their sins publicly. For penance they received a number of lashes across the back with a hickory stick. This physical punishment shocked white observers, but it maintained discipline among the band. And it made sense to warriors who were trained to tolerate physical pain without complaint. After the whipping, the sinner shook hands with the person who had whipped him.

In *Kenekuk, the Kickapoo Prophet*, historian Joseph B. Herring describes the Sunday service:

> On a typical Sunday, "criers" ran through the villages, calling believers together for services. As the people arrived, the men

moved to one side, the women to the other, the children gathered in between, and everyone stood before a roaring fire in the center of the grounds. After eating a feast prepared by Kenekuk's most devout [followers], the congregation entered the "church" and sat while the prophet [spoke], sometimes an hour or longer, followed by one or more additional speakers. When they had finished, the celebrants all shook hands and returned to their lodges.

By 1839 most of the Prairie Kickapoo had left Kansas to join their fellow tribespeople in Oklahoma, Texas, and Mexico. The Christian missionaries gave up on the Kansas Kickapoo by the early 1840s, and the U.S. government finally sent the promised money and supplies in 1843. Two years later, an Indian agent wrote that Kenekuk's people "progressed faster in civilization than any tribe I have knowledge of, particularly in agriculture." He called them "thriving and prosperous people [who are] more advanced than any other tribe" in the area.

A white official's idea of "progress" or "advancement" was not necessarily what the Indians wanted, but Kenekuk's band certainly lived more comfortably than most Indians of the mid-19th century. They grew enough food and raised enough livestock for their own needs and sold what was left over for cash. They had their own granary and a mill that was used to make flour and cut lumber. They lived in log cabins with wooden furniture.

Kenekuk died around 1852, possibly of smallpox. According to some stories, the Prophet told his followers that he would rise from the dead in three days. Many of them waited patiently beside his body, some even contracting smallpox themselves. But Kenekuk did not rise from the dead.

Without their great leader, the Kansas Kickapoo were taken advantage of by the U.S. government. Two years after Kenekuk's death, the Kickapoo were forced to sell over 600,000 acres of their tribal land. They were allowed to keep 150,000 acres, but most of this was later taken back by the government. Today descendants of Kenekuk's band still live on what is left of their land in Brown County, Kansas.

Kenekuk is one of the most interesting and unusual of the Indian spiritual leaders. He did not want to give up the traditional Indian way of life and walk the white man's road. But he was intelligent and perceptive enough to see that there were too many white men and too few Indians. He was also a truly spiritual person, who believed that peace and nonviolence was the way of the Great Spirit. Every spiritual leader dreams of a better life for his people, but Kenekuk, the Kickapoo Prophet, was one of the few whose spiritual vision led to a happier life on this earth.

SMOHALLA

◆ ◆ ◆

The Washani Prophet

Before the whites came to their land, the Indians of the Columbia River region in what is now Oregon and Washington led a good life. They ate the salmon that returned to the river every spring. They hunted game and gathered roots and berries. They performed the dances and songs and feasts of an ancient religion called *Washani* and lived under the watchful eye of the Creator.

The Columbia tribes first encountered whites when the Lewis and Clark expedition passed through the area in 1805. In the early years they were generally friendly toward the fur traders, missionaries, and settlers who followed the explorers. But later, when the intruders roared like a great white river into their land, there was trouble.

The first major conflict occurred in 1847, when a few Cayuse Indians killed a missionary named Marcus Whitman and 11 other whites because they believed Whitman had brought measles among their people. Whitman was a doctor who treated many sick whites on the Oregon Trail, and though he was not personally responsible, white diseases created devastating epidemics among the Indians.

In 1853 the United States created the Territory of Washington. Two years later, in May 1855, Territorial Governor Isaac Stevens called the Columbia River tribes to a great council at Walla Walla in southeastern Washington. Stevens tried to convince the Indians to give up their traditional lands in exchange for reservations, homes, schools, livestock, and annual payments.

Some eastern Indians who lived among the Columbia tribes told their western brothers how the government had taken their lands and forced them across the Mississippi River. There were even rumors that the government planned to remove the Columbia tribes to the Arctic. Faced with the harsh reality of U.S. policy, many tribal leaders signed the treaty of Walla Walla. But others refused to sign because they didn't trust the whites—which proved to be an accurate judgment.

Although Stevens promised that the tribes who signed could stay on their lands until the Senate ratified the treaty and the president signed it, he opened the lands to white settlement 12 days after the signing. This broken promise led to a series of bloody battles, beginning with the Yakima War in 1855.

Between 1855 and 1858, conflict and uncertainty raged across the Columbia Plateau. During this difficult time, a spiritual leader named Smohalla appeared among the Columbia River tribes. Smohalla was a member of the Wanapum, a small group related through language and culture to the larger Yakima and Walla Walla tribes. He was born at the village of Wallula on the Columbia River between 1815 and 1820.

We know nothing of Smohalla's early years, but we can assume that he learned the old ways from his parents, his relatives, and medicine people. Apparently he was born a hunchback, and this physical deformity may have set him apart as one who would walk the path of the spirit. His birth name is unknown, but some say he was called Wak-wei or Kuk-kia, which means "arising from the dust of the earth mother."

As a young man Smohalla was disturbed by the changes that he saw in his people at Wallula. They gradually forgot the old ways and the old beliefs as the intruders poured into their land. Many were drawn toward the new religion of Christianity preached by the missionaries. And right across the river was a white trading post. Smohalla despaired as he saw his people dying from white diseases, the women marrying white men, the warriors adopting white customs.

Searching for guidance, he wandered westward from the river to a sacred mountain called La Lac. There he fasted for many days until he had a vision. In *Drummers and Dreamers*, Click Relander describes Smohalla's experience:

> Every rustle of the wind or chirp of a bird spoke to him in the language of the [supernatural]. He fell asleep, the sleep of the dead; but because he was gifted, he awoke with a new song, a greater power, and instructions to add new rituals to the fragments of an old religion that had persisted through the dim years.

When Smohalla returned from the sacred mountain, he brought the symbols of a new religion: a flag with a six-pointed star that would fly during the great religious feasts—the winter dance, the first-foods feasts, and the huckleberry dance of thanksgiving; a calendar of six seasons, beginning on the winter solstice when the sun moves toward the north; and the sacred bird, Wowshuxklu, who faces the sun and tells all living things to awaken from their winter's sleep.

Whites called Smohalla's religion the Dreamer religion, because he received his revelations in a dreamlike state. In many ways, it was a revival of the old Washani religion of the Columbia River region. But Smohalla gave this old religion new life for his people.

After his experience on the sacred mountain, the young visionary discarded his birth name and took the name Shmoquala (usually written Smohalla), which means dreamer, teacher, or preacher. He became a respected *yantcha*, a spiritual leader and advisor of the Wanapum. It was said that he could understand the language of the crow and the coyote, that he could predict the coming of the salmon in the spring, and that he could foretell the death of his fellow tribespeople. Later it was said that he could predict storms, eclipses, and earthquakes.

But speaking the language of animals and telling the future was only a part of Smohalla's power. He was more than a medicine man or a magician or a psychic; he was a leader with a great vision for his people. By the 1850s Smohalla was preaching a peaceful return to traditional Indian values and a rejection of white influence. There is no evidence that Smohalla suggested violence in resisting the whites, but the spread of his teachings may have contributed to the Yakima War and other conflicts of the mid-1850s.

Smohalla's growing popularity and antiwhite teachings brought him into conflict with neighboring chiefs who believed that the best road for their people was to accept some white ways. One of these was Homily, a chief of the Walla Walla. Around 1858, Homily and Smohalla argued for three days in front of a large group of Indians gathered at Wallula.

"Return to the old tribal ways!" Smohalla cried. "Stay free of the soldiers and the reservation people . . . Unless you give up the new way, the Indian will die and there will be no full bloods among you by the time your great-grandsons are born."

Although Smohalla argued forcefully, most of the people at Wallula decided to stay with Homily and live on the reservation. In anger and frustration, Smohalla led his followers up the Columbia River to the isolated village of P'na, located at the bottom of Priest Rapids in what is now Yakima County, Washington. There they hoped to live without white influence.

At Priest Rapids, Smohalla continued to develop his faith. Although the traditional Washani religion did not include weekly worship services, Smohalla held worships every Sunday as a way of competing with the services of the Christian missionaries. The ceremonial dances and feasts were performed each year. On the days of worships or dances or feasts, Smohalla's sacred flag flew above the lodge.

As the seasons changed, Smohalla predicted the coming of the first salmon, the first roots, the first berries, or the first game. When the time of a particular food arrived, his followers brought a small amount of the food back to Priest Rapids for a feast of sharing and thanksgiving. Only when the feast was over could they obtain more of the food to feed the village. This was the old way of the Washani religion and the new way of Smohalla. For a time life was good. Then came great sorrow.

Smohalla shared his lodge at Priest Rapids with 10 wives. But with all these wives, he only had one child—a beautiful daughter. Smohalla's daughter was his most devoted follower, and he began to train her as a priestess of his religion. But when she was 15 years old, she became very ill. Smohalla used all his powers to heal her, and he called in other medicine men to help him. It was no use. His beloved daughter died.

Smohalla was so overcome with grief that he refused to leave his daughter's grave. "She is not dead, she is not dead," he wailed softly to his followers. "Leave us alone; go away and leave us alone." That evening the Prophet's followers returned to try and bring him back to the village. They found Smohalla rigid and silent, as if he had died of grief. Sadly, they carried his body back to the village and began to prepare it for burial. But the next morning he opened his eyes and rose to his knees.

For two days the Prophet refused to speak. Then he ordered his followers to prepare a feast and call the river tribes together. "I have been sent back from the Land in the Sky," he told them, "and I have brought a message for the Wanapums and the other people."

When Smohalla appeared before the river tribes he announced that he had returned from the dead with a sacred dance called the *Washat*. The Washat was an old dance of the Washani religion. But like the religion itself, the dance had been lost. Now Smohalla would teach it to the people again. And the dance would save them:

> . . . it will restore the country and the things belonging to the country to the Indians. The time is soon coming when the earth will turn over. Those of you who are pure with Indian blood and tradition will rise from the dust and float up through the earth to live forever in happiness and peace, free of oppression.

Smohalla told the people to dress in their finest clothes. Then he led them into the lodge—called a longhouse—in a special order. When everyone was inside, he selected six of the oldest and wisest men to be drummers; he himself would be the seventh drummer. He rang a bell and sang the Washat song seven times, accompanying himself with the beating of the drum:

> Sound of the bell, sound of the heart.
> My brothers.
> My sisters.
> I am meeting you.
> I am meeting you at the dance.

Smohalla gave eagle feathers to the women and white swan feathers to the men. "You are flying up, rising through the earth," he explained. "You must have the feathers when death comes or you cannot rise through the earth after the world turns over. The dance means you are climbing up; you must know how or you will stay underground forever in darkness."

Finally Smohalla showed his people the dance—the Washat—the sacred dance of the old Washani religion. Now it was the sacred dance of Smohalla's religion. That night the people danced until they collapsed from exhaustion. The following day—Sunday—they danced again. From then on, the Washat would be danced every week. It would begin on Friday and continue until Sunday night.

The Washat was the final ingredient in Smohalla's religion. With the power of the dance, the religion spread rapidly throughout the Columbia Plateau. By 1872 it was estimated that Smohalla had at least 2,000 followers. In addition he influenced many other prophets among other tribes, who developed their own versions of the new Washani religion.

Several of these prophets preached among the neighboring Nez Percé, one of the largest tribes of the Pacific Northwest. Many Nez Percé had once accepted Christianity and attempted to live peacefully with the whites. But after being cheated out of their traditional homeland, some of the tribe turned away from the white religion and adopted the new Washani faith. In 1877 Chief Joseph the Younger led the Nez Percé in a heroic, though unsuccessful, resistance against white domination called the Nez Percé War.

Although Smohalla's philosophy was nonviolent, he supported the basic ideas that the Nez Percé fought for in 1877. And the whites were more than happy to blame him for the troubles. Shortly before the war broke out, a white mob set out to lynch the Prophet while he was visiting the Yakima Reservation. But Smohalla escaped in the darkness and disappeared into the mountains.

In 1883 the opening of the Northern Pacific Railroad through the Columbia region caused new disturbances among the Indians. The following year U.S. Army Major J. W. MacMurray arrived to investigate the troubles and convince the Indians to accept individual homesteads. MacMurray visited Smohalla at Priest Rapids. Although he was a white military man who could never fully understand Smohalla or his religion, MacMurray's report provides a fascinating firsthand account of the Prophet, who was almost 70 at the time.

> In person Smohalla is peculiar. Short, thick-set, bald-headed and almost hunch-backed, he is not [impressive] at first sight, but he has an [impressively-shaped] head, with a deep brow over bright, intelligent eyes. He is a finished orator. His manner is mostly of the bland, insinuating, persuasive style, but when aroused he is full of fire . . . His audience seemed spellbound under his magic manner, and it never lost interest to me, though he spoke in a language comprehended by few white men and translated to me at second or third hand.

During his stay at Priest Rapids, MacMurray had the rare opportunity to observe the spiritual leader in his dreamlike states:

> He falls into trances and lies rigid for considerable periods. Unbelievers have experimented by sticking needles through his flesh, cutting him with knives, and otherwise testing his sensibility to pain, without provoking any responsive action. It was asserted that he was surely dead, because blood did not flow from his wounds. These trances always excite great interest and often alarm, as he threatens to abandon his earthly body altogether because of the disobedience of his people.

The main cause of the Indian-white conflicts in the Columbia region was the question of land ownership. As Smohalla and his followers listened, MacMurray explained the Indian Homestead Law and the way in which the whites divided the land. He encouraged the Indians to apply for individual homesteads and to settle on them as soon as possible. Smohalla replied that he knew all about these laws, but that they were against the laws of the earth.

The Prophet began his explanation with the story of creation. According to Smohalla, *Nami Piap* created all men and women with wings, and people could fly anywhere. The rivers were full of salmon, the plains were full of buffalo, and there was plenty for

Smohalla and his priests. This photograph was taken around 1884, probably during Major MacMurray's visit to Priest Rapids. (National Anthropological Archives, Smithsonian Institution)

everyone to eat. But then the strong began to oppress the weak and claim the best land for their own. Smohalla continued:

> [Nami Piap] was very angry at this, and he took away their wings and commanded that the lands and fisheries should be common to all who lived upon them; that they were never to be marked off or divided, but that the people should enjoy the fruits that [Nami Piap] planted in the land, and the animals that lived upon it, and the fishes in the water . . . This is the old law . . . Those who cut up the lands or sign papers for lands will be defrauded of their rights and will be punished by [Nami Piap's] anger.

Smohalla said that Nami Piap was the father of all things and the earth was the mother of humankind. He was against farming or mining because it was like destroying his mother's body:

You ask me to plow the ground! Shall I take a knife and tear my mother's bosom? Then when I die she will not take me to her bosom to rest.

You ask me to dig for stone! Shall I dig under her skin for bones? Then when I die I cannot enter her body to be born again.

You ask me to cut grass and make hay and sell it, and be rich like white men! But how dare I cut off my mother's hair?

As the years passed, many of Smohalla's younger followers drifted away—some to live on reservations, some to farm their own homesteads, some to ride the range as cowboys or to find other work in the white man's world. His older followers died, and the devoted group at Priest Rapids grew smaller and smaller. Smohalla became blind and weak in body, but he continued to dream and preach until his death around 1895.

His son, Yoyouni—born after the death of Smohalla's beloved daughter—carried on his father's work until his own death in 1917. Smohalla's nephew, Puck Hyah Toot—who was called the Last Prophet—preached the religion and danced the Washat until his death around 1965. Today the Wanapums at Priest Rapids and other Indians of the Columbia Plateau continue Smohalla's faith. On some reservations it is called the Seven Drums Religion.

Smohalla was one of many dreamer-prophets who preached in the Columbia River region during the 19th century. Like Smohalla, most of these leaders visited another world and returned with songs, dances, and ceremonies for their people. But Smohalla was the most important and influential of the dreamer-prophets. For it was Smohalla who first revived the Washat, the sacred dance of the old Washani religion. And it was Smohalla who combined the old ways with a new vision, creating a religion that gave his people strength and comfort in the face of the white intruders.

JOHN SLOCUM

◆ ◆ ◆

The Shaker Prophet

In the second half of the 19th century, the Indians who lived near Puget Sound in Washington State suffered under white control. Some of their suffering was physical—white diseases ravaged them and reservations confined them. But the worst suffering was social and spiritual. Government agents and Christian ministers forced them to give up their traditional way of life and religious beliefs, encouraging them to live and pray like whites. But the white man's road did not make the Indians happy.

The pale-skinned newcomers were not the only problem for the Puget Sound Indians. They also suffered at the hands of the traditional Indian doctors, or shamans. The Indians believed that these doctors could poison their victims by shooting their guardian spirits into the victim's body. The doctors could also heal the sick, but they demanded high payment for their services.

In this atmosphere of social breakdown and fear of Indian doctors, a new religion was born. It began with a man named John Slocum, who lived on southwestern Puget Sound at an inlet called Skookum Chuck. We know little about Slocum before 1881. Around 40 years old at that time, he was a member of the Squaxin band, part of the large Salish Indian group of the Pacific Northwest.

Outwardly, Slocum was a very ordinary man: about 5' 8" tall, stoop-shouldered, with a head that had been flattened at birth—a traditional practice of his people. He was soft-spoken and humble.

He and his wife Mary had 13 children, but only two—both daughters—lived to adulthood. Slocum supported his family with a small logging operation in the forests around his home. Like many other Indians in the area, he smoked, drank a little, and gambled too much. He was especially fond of betting on Indian pony races.

Then, in the late fall of 1881, something amazing happened. There are many versions of the story, but they all agree on the essential facts: John Slocum "died," went to heaven, and returned with a message for his people—a message that would change their lives.

One eyewitness reported that John broke his neck in a logging accident but that Slocum's father believed the accident was actually caused by an Indian doctor. Slocum was carried back to his house, where his family washed and dressed his body for burial and covered him with a white sheet. His two half-brothers set out in a canoe to buy a coffin in the nearby town of Olympia.

After a few hours, John began to move beneath the sheet. As his family and the other mourners watched with wonder and fear, he pulled the sheet away from his face, turned his head from side to side, stretched his arms, and sat up. Walking outside, he took off his clothes, washed with clean water, and wrapped himself in a clean sheet. He ordered his wife to throw away his burial clothes and the old sheet because they were things of his death.

When he came back inside, John asked everyone in the room to shake hands with him. Then he asked them to kneel with him and began to pray. He announced that he had died and gone to the gates of heaven—the Christian heaven—where he met an angel who sent him back to earth with a message for the Indians.

They must stop smoking, drinking, gambling, and practicing Indian shamanism. They must pray and cross themselves every morning and evening and before meals. They must attend regular church services and build a church for John to preach in and continue his teachings. If they did these things, God would give them a great "medicine" to help them.

Ten years later, John Slocum told his own version of the story through an interpreter:

... All at once I saw a shining light—great light—trying my soul. I looked and saw my body had no soul—looked at my own body—it was dead ... When I saw it, it was pretty poor. My soul left body and went up to judgment place of God ...

I have seen a great light in my soul from that good land; I have understood all Christ wants us to do. Before I came alive I saw I was sinner. Angel in heaven said to me, "You must go back and turn alive again on earth." I learned that I must be good Christian man on earth, or will be punished ... When I came back, I told my friends, "There is a God—there is a Christian people. My good friends, be Christian."

When I came alive, I tell my friends, "Good thing in heaven. God is kind to us. If you all try hard and help me we will be better men on earth." And now we all feel that it is so.

John's family and neighbors built him a church—some say in four days, others say in four weeks. On the appointed day the roof was not finished, so they stretched a tarp across the open space and John began to preach. His teachings were primarily Christian—that God is good and all-powerful, that He will help human beings who avoid sin and pray to Him regularly, and that His Son, Jesus Christ, lived on earth and will return again.

Although these teachings are common to all Christian churches, Slocum was influenced most by the Catholic religion. In fact there is evidence that he was actually baptized in the Catholic Church shortly before his "death." When he preached, he wore a long white shirt with the tails out, a garment similar to a priest's vestment. And he placed special importance on the sign of the cross, bells and candles, and long periods of silent, kneeling prayer—all more typical of Catholic than Protestant churches.

The story of John Slocum's supernatural experience created great excitement in the southern Puget Sound area. Although Slocum's message was not that different from the teachings of the white missionaries, the fact that a local Indian had a direct experience in the Christian heaven made a strong impression on people who were looking for their own religious identity.

A few years earlier, an Indian named Big Bill had begun a religious movement on the Skokomish Reservation, 12 miles north of Skookum Chuck. Big Bill prophesied that someone in the area would receive great power from God and that the people should help him and believe him. Big Bill had died in June 1881, and when John Slocum returned from the dead that fall, the Skokomish Indians believed it was the fulfillment of Big Bill's prophecy.

After a few months, however, the initial excitement over John Slocum's revelations began to die down. Slocum himself seemed to forget his own teachings, sliding back to his old sinful ways— especially his fondness for gambling. Then in 1882, about a year after his first experience, John Slocum almost died again. This time the cause was apparently sickness, but once again his father believed the real problem was an evil Indian doctor. He insisted on hiring another Indian doctor to try and save his son.

John Slocum had preached against Indian doctors, and his wife Mary was one his strongest disciples. Even when John forgot his own teachings, Mary continued to follow them, and she was disturbed that her husband was under the power of an Indian doctor. One day, in hysterics, she ran down to a creek near their house and began to wash her face. Suddenly she collapsed, and her family and friends carried her back to the house.

When she regained consciousness, Mary began to moan and tremble. Her hands shook uncontrollably, and the shaking soon spread throughout her body. She insisted that John be removed from the hut of the Indian doctor and brought into the house. The onlookers were so amazed by Mary's strange appearance that they obeyed her and laid John's body in the center of the room, with blood pouring from his nose. Mary ordered some of her relatives to stand in various positions around him, holding candles in their hands and extending their arms over his body.

In *Indian Shakers,* author H. G. Barnett describes what happened next, as told to him by Mary Slocum's sister, Annie James:

> Mary gave Henry [her brother] a hand bell that Slocum used in his religious services and told him to ring it. At first "he was bashful," but after a while he began to twitch and jump just as Mary was doing. Before long the two other women [Mary's mother and sister-in-law] were doing the same. In the meantime Mary prayed fervently calling upon God and Jesus to spare her husband's life, and repeating from time to time in a sobbing voice: "He is going to

live. He is going to live. Jesus will save him. Jesus will save him."
No one knows how long this performance continued, but when it
was over Slocum's nose had ceased to bleed. It had stopped mirac-
ulously.

This was the beginning of shaking.

John Slocum recovered from his illness and returned to the
Christian path. At first he was suspicious of shaking, because he
thought it might be from the devil. But gradually he accepted it
and decided that shaking was the powerful "medicine" that the
angel had promised him in his original vision.

The religious excitement returned to southern Puget Sound,
even stronger than before. Indians came to Skookum Chuck and
caught "the shake" from Mary and Henry and others. "You never
had to give the power to them in those days," Annie James
remembered. "It just came. It was catching, like the measles."

With the introduction of shaking, John Slocum's importance in
the new religion declined. In the beginning Slocum had experienced God's power directly, and only by listening to his teachings
could the other Indians share in the experience. But with shaking,
anyone could directly experience God. John Slocum was still
honored as the original prophet, but it is not clear whether he ever
actually caught "the shake" himself.

For the next year, Mary Slocum was the center of the growing
religion. However, Mary soon found herself in conflict with another of John's early disciples, Louis Yowaluch, called Mud Bay
Louis because he lived on Mud Bay of Puget Sound. Like her
husband, Mary Slocum was a simple person who saw the power
of shaking in simple, humble terms. Louis had bigger visions. He
emphasized the end of the world and the second coming of Christ.
He was more influenced by Protestant religion than by Catholicism, and he had his own ideas about the right way to hold
services.

The conflict came to a head in August 1883, when hundreds of
Indians arrived for a religious meeting at John Slocum's church.
The meeting went on for a week, with Indians praying, shaking,
and curing. According to some stories, four women tried to be-

come angels and some people died while attempting supernatural feats.

Louis Yowaluch left in the middle of the meeting and returned with his followers to his house on Mud Bay. There he continued to hold services, and in time he built his own church. Although Mary and John Slocum remained active in the Shaker religion, Mud Bay Louis now emerged as the true leader.

The big meeting attracted the attention of the Indian agent at the Skokomish Reservation, Edwin Eells, and his brother Myron, who was a Protestant missionary. For the next several years, the Eells brothers did everything in their power to stop the growth of the new religion. At one point they jailed Shaker leaders—including John Slocum and Louis Yowaluch—for seven weeks, forcing them to work along the roadside in chains while other Indians made fun of them, and then forcing them to sit in the front row of the Presbyterian church on Sundays.

Despite the opposition of the Eells brothers and other white authorities, the Shaker religion continued to grow. Many converts were drawn by the healing power of the Shakers, as well as by their success at finding lost objects and predicting the future. Unlike the Indian doctors, the Shakers offered these services freely. They believed their supernatural powers came directly from God, and they used these powers only for good.

The persecution of the Shakers ended in 1892, when a white lawyer named James Wickersham helped them to organize as a legal church. A few years earlier, in 1887, the U.S. Congress had passed the Dawes Severalty Act, which provided that any Indian who settled on an individual parcel of land and lived in a "civilized" manner would be considered a U.S. citizen with the same rights and privileges as any other citizen. Wickersham explained to the Shakers that this meant they had the freedom to worship God in any way they chose.

On June 6, 1892, the Shaker leaders met at Louis Yowaluch's house at Mud Bay. With Wickersham's help, they officially organized themselves as the Indian Shaker Church. Louis Yowaluch was elected "headman." Seven elders and five ministers were also elected, with Louis Yowaluch and John Slocum being elected to

John Slocum and Louis Yowaluch (l to r). This photograph was sent to the Bureau of American Ethnology in November 1892 by James Wickersham, the attorney who provided legal advice to the early Indian Shaker Church. The raised right hand was a symbolic Shaker gesture. (National Anthropological Archives, Smithsonian Institution)

both positions. Mary Slocum was offered a position as minister, but she declined—probably because of the old conflict with Louis.

At first the white residents of Puget Sound were disturbed by the idea of an Indian Christian church with Indian officers, Indian preachers, and buildings built by Indians. But with Wickersham's legal support, the Indian Shaker Church was never seriously challenged again.

John Slocum died sometime between 1896 and 1898. Louis Yowaluch continued to lead the church until his own death in 1905. Two years later Louis's brother, Mud Bay Sam, was elected headman. In 1910 the Shakers reorganized as an official corporation in the state of Washington, with a hierarchy that was similar to a Protestant church. Mud Bay Sam was elected the first bishop.

During the 1920s and 1930s, the Shaker Church was torn apart by a conflict over the Bible. The original Shaker leaders—John Slocum, Mary Slocum, Mud Bay Louis, and Mud Bay Sam—could not read or write. They believed that the Bible was a good book for the whites, but that the Indians could experience God's truth directly, first through John Slocum's "death" and later through shaking. However, as more educated Indians joined the church, they wanted to read the Bible during their services. The older Shakers fought this new idea.

The conflict led to a split within the church in 1944. The anti-Bible group continued as the Indian Shaker Church, while the Bible-reading group called themselves the Indian Full Gospel Church. Both these churches still exist today in congregations throughout the Pacific Northwest, from British Columbia to northern California. During the 1970s there were almost 1,000 active, practicing Shakers in the two denominations. However, thousands of other Indians and whites have been touched by the Shakers—either through their cures or through the example of their good, honest lives.

Shaker churches are simple wooden buildings with a bell tower above the entrance. Inside, a prayer table covered with a white cloth holds the bells and candles that are used in the service. Crosses and Christian pictures decorate the walls. The participants sit on benches along the walls in the front half of the church—men and boys on one side, women and girls on the other side, with a big open space between them. Benches for onlookers fill the back of the church.

At the Sunday morning worship service, the Shakers wear long white robes with a cross made of blue ribbon on the front. The service begins with a prayer by the minister or another member of the congregation, followed by a sermon. Then the congregation sings to the rhythm of handbells as they march in a counterclockwise circle three times around the open space. The service ends with each member of the congregation touching hands with every other member in a special pattern.

Although there is some shaking at the Sunday services, the real shaking occurs at evening curing ceremonies called "shakes." New converts or people seeking help stand in the center of the open space as the Shakers circle around them or march in place to the rhythm of the handbells. Gradually some of the participants begin to shake and tremble as they "get the power." To heal a sick or troubled person, a Shaker may try to brush or fan the sin away with his hands, pass a lighted candle over the person's body, or direct the sound of a handbell at the sufferer. Afterward, the Shaker may explain what he or she believes to be the problem for that particular person and suggest a solution.

The Indian Shaker Church is a unique, original religious movement. It has no connection with the 18th-century English church, the United Society of Believers, who were commonly called Shakers. It is also very different from other Indian spiritual revivals. On one level, John Slocum's "death and resurrection" is similar to the experience of Indian prophets such as Handsome Lake, Tenskwatawa, Smohalla, and Wovoka. But these prophets preached a message of return to traditional Indian values and rejection of white culture. John Slocum and the other Shaker leaders took the opposite approach. They rejected traditional Indian practices, especially shamanism, and embraced the white man's Christianity— but they did it in a way that made sense to them as Indians.

In her article "The Indian Shaker Church," Pamela T. Amoss explains the historical importance of the Shakers:

> The position of the church in local Indian history is unique. It was the first fully Indian institution to achieve legal respectability in the eyes of the dominant [white] society at a time when other forms of Indian spiritual expression were actively suppressed . . . Shakerism affirmed the principle of Indians working together to help each other against the specters of illness and sin.

Although the growth of the church was due primarily to the efforts of Louis Yowaluch and his followers, Louis always honored and respected John Slocum as the prophet who brought the good news from heaven. He said, "We heard there was a God from Slocum—we could see it. Same time we heard God, we believe it . . . John Slocum brought good to us; his words civilized us."

Louis's brother, Mud Bay Sam, put it this way: "Among the Shakers, John Slocum is first."

ZOTOM

◆ ◆ ◆

Warrior, Artist, Missionary, and Seeker

During the mid-19th century, the Kiowa ranged over what is now Oklahoma and northern Texas. Like the Comanche—their allies to the south—the Kiowa were expert horsemen and fearless raiders. Together the two tribes dominated vast areas of the southern Plains, hunting buffalo, battling their traditional Indian enemies, raiding in Mexico, and fighting against white settlement in Texas.

Although the Indians resisted white settlement, they could not resist the new diseases the whites brought with them. From the late 1840s to the 1870s, a series of epidemics ravaged the Kiowa and Comanche, weakening the once-powerful "Lords of the Southern Plains." In 1867 the tribes yielded to U.S. government pressure and signed the Treaty of Medicine Lodge, trading their traditional land for a reservation in southwestern Indian Territory (present-day Oklahoma) while keeping the right to hunt on the Staked Plain—a rugged plateau in the Texas Panhandle.

Although most Kiowa settled on the reservation, warriors crossed the reservation boundaries to continue their traditional hunting and raiding. In January 1871 a small Kiowa raiding party killed four teamsters hauling supplies along the Butterfield Trail in northern Texas. Shortly afterward the Kiowa stole a herd of horses in a nearby county. Later that spring a larger Kiowa-Comanche raiding party attacked another wagon train along the Butterfield Trail, killed six teamsters, and captured 40 mules.

A young warrior named Zotom participated in the first two Kiowa raids and probably joined in the raid on the wagon train as well. Born in 1853, Zotom was only 18 at the time of the raids. We know little of his early life, but his father was a full-blooded Kiowa named Keintikeah (White Shield) and his mother was a half-Kiowa, half-Crow named Sahpooly (Owl). He had four younger brothers. The name Zotom means "Biter" or "Hole-bite," but the significance of the name is unknown.

With his fierce spirit, keen intelligence, and muscular physique, Zotom was well-suited for the life of a Kiowa warrior. Had he been born in an earlier time, he might have become a great war leader of his people. But Zotom came of age as a warrior at a time when the Kiowa and Comanche were fighting a last desperate battle for their traditional life—a life that depended on the great herds of buffalo that once roamed the southern Plains.

For years the tribes had watched as white hunters slowly depleted the herds. But now they realized that something new was happening—a wholesale slaughter on the southern Plains. In the past, white hunters had killed buffalo for hides only during the winter months, when their fur was long. But by 1870 a new tanning method had been developed to process short-haired summer hides. Railroads extending into Kansas offered a cheap way of shipping the hides to market. And high-powered telescopic rifles allowed the hunters to kill the great beasts from a distance of 600 yards.

In June of 1874 the Comanche and Kiowa held a sun dance—the great religious ceremony of the Plains Indians. Although the Kiowa performed the sun dance each year, the Comanche did not follow the sun dance tradition. Now, however, the tribes performed the dance together and invited their traditional enemies from the north, the Cheyenne and Arapaho, to join them. The time for fighting each other was past; it was time to fight the white buffalo hunters.

After the ceremony the four tribes formed a force of 700 warriors—including Zotom—under the leadership of the Comanche chief, Quanah Parker. On June 16, 1874, the Indians attacked a group of 28 white buffalo hunters at Adobe Walls, an abandoned trading post in the Texas Panhandle. Although vastly out-numbered, the buffalo hunters held off the Indian attack with high-powered rifles and a huge supply of ammunition.

This began a series of conflicts called the Red River War or the Buffalo War. Throughout the summer the Indians raided white settlements and skirmished with federal soldiers. The turning point came on September 28, 1874, when soldiers under Colonel Ranald Mackenzie attacked the Indians in Palo Duro Canyon, a fortresslike stronghold on the Staked Plain. Although Mackenzie's men killed only three warriors, they captured or killed most of their horses and destroyed their tipis and food supplies.

A month later, warriors began trickling in to surrender at Fort Reno and Fort Sill in the Indian Territory. Throughout the harsh winter that followed, federal soldiers pursued the remaining war-riors relentlessly. Zotom was among the last group of Kiowa warriors arrested on February 18, 1875. Quanah Parker and a group of Comanche held out the longest, finally surrendering on June 2.

Even before Quanah's surrender, white officials were deter-mined to destroy the seeds of the Indian uprising. They decided to send the most "dangerous" warriors to prison at Fort Marion in St. Augustine, Florida—over 1,200 miles from their old life on the southern Plains. A Kiowa "peace-chief" identified Zotom and the other warriors to the federal soldiers. The informer was later killed by his own people.

In April 1875, 72 Indians were chained into wagons at Fort Sill and carried away to begin their long journey, most of it by railroad. On May 21, the prisoners arrived at their final destination. Sidney Lanier, a white poet who saw the prisoners arrive, described them with a mixture of pity and respect:

> I saw seventy-two big Indians yesterday: proper men and tall, as one would wish to behold. They were weary and greatly worn; but as they stepped out of the [train] cars, and folded their ample blankets around them, there was a large dignity and majestic sweep

about their movements that made me much desire to salute their grave excellencies. Each had his ankles chained together; but managed to walk like a man, withal. They are confined—by some ass who is in authority—in the lovely old Fort, as unfit for them as they for it. It is in my heart to hope sincerely that they may all get out.

Although Lanier's description is sympathetic, his arithmetic was slightly off. One of the 72 prisoners—a Cheyenne chief named Grey Beard—had jumped from the train that very morning, preferring to die rather than live in chains. Grey Beard survived the jump, but he was found by a guard, who shot him on the spot despite orders to deliver the Indians alive.

When he first arrived at Fort Marion, Zotom was so angry and rebellious that the prison commander, Captain Richard H. Pratt, threw him into the dark, damp dungeon of the old stone fortress. Years later, when Zotom returned to his people after imprisonment and education in the white man's world, an article in a church magazine described his early problems—as well as his extraordinary character:

> This man for months after his capture was so perverse and insubordinate that it was almost determined to shoot him as an example to his companions of the necessity of submission to authority. Strong, self-willed, passionate, he has fought many a hard battle with [him]self in his upward climbing, and has doubtless many a one yet to fight . . . ardent, impulsive, fearless, of diversified and brilliant gifts.

The idea of "upward climbing" reflects the 19th-century attitude toward the Indians, particularly the attitude of reformers who genuinely wanted to help them. Today we would consider this attitude racist, because it assumes that the Indians' traditional way of life was "lower" than the white way of life. But at the time, the idea that the Indians should be educated to be more like whites was more humane than the opposing idea—that the only good Indian was a dead Indian.

The commander of Fort Marion, Captain Pratt, believed strongly in educating his Indian prisoners. He began by instructing them in English, and with the help of volunteers from St.

Augustine, he soon had a regular school operating within the prison, teaching the "three Rs" of reading, writing, and arithmetic. Pratt provided instruction in a fourth "R" as well: religion. Although reformers like Pratt respected the Indians' personal qualities, they believed that Indian religion was "pagan" and that Christianity offered the only possible salvation.

We don't know how long Pratt kept Zotom in the dungeon, but when he reemerged into the light of day he became a model prisoner of many talents. He progressed quickly in his studies, and he was a wonderful dancer who entertained tourists and visiting officials. He was also a fine singer and a bugler who sounded the call for various prison duties. But Zotom's greatest talent at Fort Marion was as an artist.

Shortly after they arrived, the prisoners made bows and arrows and other traditional items to sell to tourists. Pratt decided to encourage their artistic talents by providing them with sketchbooks, drawing pencils, and colored ink. The experiment was a great success—at least 26 of the prisoners produced artistic work. Much of this art was sold to tourists, while other work was kept by Pratt or sent to military and government officials as proof that his efforts at "reform" were succeeding.

Over a century later, about 745 pieces of art from Fort Marion still survive. Of these, 108 are credited to Zotom. Zotom was especially in demand for his ability to decorate ladies' fans, but he also produced a number of impressive sketchbooks. In fact, Harriet Beecher Stowe—the famous author of *Uncle Tom's Cabin*—was so impressed with one of Zotom's sketchbooks that she bought it and asked him to make another just like it. Captain Pratt had to write Stowe to apologize for Zotom's slow work on the second sketchbook, because he was too busy decorating ladies' fans.

Like the work of the other artists, Zotom's art grew directly out of the traditional pictographic hide-painting of the Plains Indians, in which certain pictures represented certain words or ideas. On the Plains, pictography was used to record the exploits of a great warrior or the history of a tribe. However, in the prison of Fort Marion, far away from their old life, the artists developed their traditional pictography into a new art form. In *Plains Indian*

Art from Fort Marion, Karen Daniels Peterson discusses this development:

> In Fort Marion, with the old societal structure shattered, drawing passed from the social to the personal. A new concept entered pictorial drawing—self expression, art for art's sake. The artists . . . were free to concentrate on pictures appealing to the eye and to the emotions. The Plains Indians . . . crossed over the bridge to the era of modern Indian art when the prisoners in irons shuffled across the drawbridge to shed their chains at Fort Marion.

In April 1878, after three years in Fort Marion, the Indian prisoners were released. Although most returned to their reservations, Zotom and 21 other young men chose to stay in the East for further education. The only school that would accept the Indian pupils was Hampton Institute, a segregated school for blacks in Virginia. However, Zotom and three other top students were chosen to study for the Episcopal ministry in New York State.

The idea of training the Indians as ministers had been developed by an Episcopal deaconess named Mary D. Burnham. The four ministry candidates stayed with Burnham in Syracuse, New York for several weeks of preparation and then moved on to the small town of Paris in the beautiful countryside south of Utica. There they lived and studied with the family of Reverend John B. Wicks. Wicks and his wife treated the young Indians as sons, and their pupils responded with genuine affection and hard work.

On October 6, 1878, the four ministry candidates were baptized at Grace Episcopal Church in Syracuse, New York. Zotom chose the Christian name Paul Caryl Zotom. The name "Paul" honored Saint Paul, who laid the foundations of Christianity. The name "Caryl" honored Harriet E. Caryl, an officer of an Episcopal women's organization that provided his financial support. Two weeks after their baptism, the candidates were confirmed.

As they progressed in their studies, Reverend Wicks had great hopes for his pupils, especially Zotom. In a report to his superiors, Wicks described Zotom's character, personality, and intelligence:

The Kiowa [Zotom], after his own kind, quick to see, apt to learn, sometimes headstrong and sometimes heartstrong is growing in his own way. Of the four, he will be the voice which shall tell out with all the grace of Indian eloquence the good tidings that are now coming to him, and through him to his people.

On June 7, 1881, after three years of study, Zotom was ordained as a deacon in the Episcopal Church. The Cheyenne candidate, David Pendleton (Making Medicine), was also ordained, but the Comanche candidate, Henry Pratt (Buffalo Scout), was not considered ready. The fourth candidate had died the previous year. Zotom read the Gospel at the ordination ceremony, and according to the Episcopal bishop, "His clear, rich voice filled the church, and every listener's heart thrilled with emotion."

After the ceremony, Reverend Wicks and his three pupils boarded a train for the Indian Territory. Wicks and David Pendleton would establish a mission among the Cheyenne, while Zotom and Henry Pratt would establish a mission among the Kiowa and Comanche. When Zotom and Pratt arrived at the Anadarko Agency on June 17, they were the only missionaries among the Kiowa, Comanche, or Kiowa-Apache. Thus they faced no competition from other Christian groups. Instead, they faced a more powerful competition from the traditional religion of their own people.

At the time of their arrival, the Kiowa were preparing to move to the sacred grounds for the sun dance. The dance was always a time of great excitement, but this year the excitement was even greater because a young medicine man had predicted that he would bring the buffalo back out of the earth during the dance. Over 1,400 Kiowa assembled on the sacred grounds in mid-July. By this time, Reverend Wicks had come to check on Zotom's progress. Wicks decided that Zotom should set up a "Christian tent" on the grounds. "Here morning and evening should be a gathering for prayer, with instruction through the day to as many as would assemble."

Zotom stayed on the sacred grounds during the last 10 days of preparation and the first night of the four-day dance. It is unclear exactly what happened during this period, but rumors quickly circulated that Zotom had ripped off his white man's clothes, stripped to a G-string, and joined the dance. Zotom denied these rumors, and the fact that he left after the first night of dancing suggests he might have been "turning away from temptation." However, after six years in the East, it would certainly be understandable if Zotom felt a powerful desire to join the traditional religious ceremony of his people.

Although the government agent was not present at the dance, he reported Zotom's "bad behavior" to his old jailer, Captain Pratt, who was now head of a school for Indian students. Pratt passed on the report to the Commissioner of Indian Affairs in Washington, D.C. This created a great stir and got Zotom's Christian ministry off to a rocky start. However, Reverend Wicks and Deaconess Burnham never wavered in their support of their prize pupil. In a letter to Burnham, Zotom defended his behavior in English that was slightly ungrammatical but heartfelt and eloquent:

> I am sorry that you hear about me that I have on Indian clothes. It is not so, dear House Mother, the white men tell you a lie. I thought myself I doing very well here. I teach them all the boys, and preach on Sunday. I go and pray with the sick. Nobody here doing the good way; but I try.

By the following year, Wicks reported that Zotom was making progress with Sunday school classes and that he had even convinced one of his relatives—a traditional Kiowa medicine man—to give up the "devil medicine" and accept the white man's religion. Upon hearing of Zotom's progress, Captain Pratt admitted that he might have made a mistake and judged him too harshly.

For several years Zotom continued to follow the path of a Christian deacon. In April 1882, he married a Christian Comanche woman named Mary. They had three children, but all of them died in childhood. (Before his imprisonment, he had been married to a Kiowa woman with whom he had a son who lived to adulthood.) Zotom was especially successful with his younger brothers, convincing them to cut their long hair, wear white-style clothing, and either work or attend school.

In 1884, however, Zotom faced a difficult test of his new beliefs. After three years in the Indian Territory, Reverend Wicks returned to the East because of poor health. Although Zotom had been in charge of the Kiowa mission, Wicks visited him often and provided fatherly advice and guidance. In a letter to Wicks, Zotom expressed his deep respect and concern:

> Mr. Wicks, I am very sorry you not come any more to Anadarko. When I read your letter make me feel very sorry and come down my tears a great deal, because I think I can't any man find like Mr. Wicks. I thought Mr. Wicks stay with me always and never go way anywhere. And now he is gone away off. I can't see him anymore. Now, I say good-by. God bless you . . . I know somebody stay with me. I mean our father in heaven.

Although Zotom requested that the church send another missionary to help him, he was left alone—literally a voice in the wilderness. Apparently he slipped away from his missionary work fairly quickly. A year and a half after Wicks's departure, another Indian artist from Fort Marion reported, "The Kiowas, Comanches, and [Kiowa-] Apaches have no missionaries, nobody to teach them about God's ways." In 1888 an Indian Presbyterian missionary visited Zotom at his home and reported, "He allowed his hair to grow long and is now a leading medicine man."

Disturbed by these reports, an Episcopal bishop visited the Indian Territory in July 1889. He stopped first at the Cheyenne mission, where he found that David Pendleton was still walking the Christian road after five years on his own: " . . . he has the confidence of all, both Indians and whites . . . I found that the Cheyenne Deacon had been faithful in performing such duties as he could." In fact David Pendleton served faithfully as a Christian missionary for 50 years.

Paul Zotom was a different story. The bishop arrived at the Anadarko Agency and asked to see his deacon. Five days later, Zotom arrived, and the bishop described their meeting in his diary for Wednesday, July 17:

Today the Rev. Paul Zotom, who has been since Monday after-
noon in the neighborhood, made his first appearance, and his
costume differed in no essential respect from that worn by the
Indians in camp. It is true that his face was not painted, but this
was about the only thing which distinguished him from the great
body of the Kiowas. He has evidently left the "white man's road,"
and returned to the Indian path.

After his meeting with Zotom, the bishop placed him on the list of
retired ministers and stopped payment of his $300 annual salary.

A year later, a great new religion swept across the Plains from
Texas to the Dakotas. It was called the Ghost Dance, and it began
with the visions of a Northern Paiute Indian named Wovoka.
Although the Ghost Dance became most powerful among the
Lakota (Teton Sioux), the Kiowa, Arapaho, Cheyenne, and some
Comanche were also strong believers. The dance offered hope
of a new world where they would see their dead relatives and
once again hunt the endless herds of buffalo. (For more information on the Ghost Dance, see the profile of Wovoka on page 80.)

We do not know if Zotom participated in the Ghost Dance,
but considering his life of spiritual seeking, it seems likely that
he did. His wife, Mary, became a true believer who composed a
well-known Ghost Song used in the dance. Unfortunately, the
Ghost Dance ended in disappointment and tragedy—disappointment when the dead relatives and buffalo did not return; tragedy
when federal soldiers killed over 150 Lakota at Wounded Knee.

In 1893, two years after the Ghost Dance died out, Zotom
divorced Mary and married another Christian woman named
Mary Aungattay. They had no children. The following year, on
August 13, 1894, a new bishop formally deposed Zotom as an
Episcopal deacon after Zotom wrote him a letter giving up the
ministry. However, he had not yet given up on Christianity. In
1895 he was baptized into the Baptist religion, and the following
spring Zotom and his new wife helped a Baptist missionary,
Isabel Crawford, establish a mission among the Kiowa. Zotom
acted as Crawford's interpreter and helped her convert many of
his fellow tribespeople. However, Zotom's own enthusiasm for
the Baptist faith did not last.

Zotom painting a model tipi for the Smithsonian exhibit at the Trans-Mississippi and International Exposition. Photograph by anthropologist James Mooney at Anadarko, Indian Territory in 1897. (National Anthropological Archives, Smithsonian Institution)

By 1897 he had left Crawford's mission and returned to the Anadarko Agency, where he created his first known artwork since leaving Fort Marion. The anthropologist James Mooney, who studied the Ghost Dance and was well-respected among the Plains tribes, commissioned Zotom to paint a series of model tipis for a Smithsonian exhibit at the Trans-Mississippi and International Exposition to be held in Omaha the following year. At the agency, Zotom also returned to his old talents as a bugler.

Around this time—after years of spiritual searching—Zotom

finally found satisfaction in the peyote religion. Peyote is a small spineless cactus that grows near the border of Mexico and Texas. Eating the top of the cactus—called the peyote button—produces visions and a feeling of strength and well-being. In its native area peyote has been used for medicinal and spiritual purposes for thousands of years. However, it was only during the 1870s that peyotism spread northward to the Indian Territory. By that time, Christian ideas had become mixed with traditional Indian beliefs in the all-night peyote ceremony.

We do not know the details of Zotom's participation in the peyote religion. But it is not hard to understand why it offered him something that other religions lacked. Born a free Kiowa warrior, he could never turn away completely from the traditions of his people. But after years of Christian education and work as a Christian missionary, he could not turn away completely from Christianity either. He was caught between two worlds, and the peyote religion allowed him to live in both worlds at once—to be a Christian and an Indian at the same time.

Zotom died at the age of 60 on April 27, 1913. In his later years, he lost the muscular, athletic body of his youth and became obese—one observer estimated that he weighed 325 pounds, and he had a reputation for eating and drinking too much. Though this behavior was unhealthy, it fit the personality of this brilliant, talented man. Everything Zotom did, he did with passion: fighting, raiding, hunting, drawing, dancing, singing, preaching, and searching for God.

WOVOKA

◆ ◆ ◆

The Ghost Dance Prophet

In 1890 a great spiritual movement swept across the West like a raging prairie fire. From California to South Dakota, Indians of over 30 tribes performed a sacred dance—holding hands, singing holy songs, and shuffling their feet in a circle. It was called the Ghost Dance because some dancers believed that they would see their dead relatives in visions during the dance.

There were other beliefs too, and the beliefs varied from tribe to tribe. Some said that an Indian Messiah was coming to drive the whites from the land and create a new earth, where the Indians would be forever young and the buffalo would once again thunder across the Plains. Others said that the Messiah was already upon the earth, and that he was a western Indian called a "fish-eater."

The 1890 Ghost Dance was the most powerful Indian religious movement since the coming of the white intruders. It united Indians who spoke many different languages and held different spiritual beliefs. The idea of Indian unity created hysteria among the whites, who feared that the Ghost Dances were war dances leading to an Indian uprising. This hysteria exploded in tragedy when federal soldiers killed over 150 Lakota men, women, and children at Wounded Knee in South Dakota.

Even before the tragedy of Wounded Knee, white authorities had begun to ask the question: Who is this Indian Messiah? Or—to quote an American army officer—this "Indian who impersonated Christ." Today, more than a century later, this is still an important question. And an equally important question is: What were the original teachings of the 1890 Ghost Dance? The answer to both these questions lies in the life of an extraordinary man named Wovoka.

Wovoka was born around 1856 or 1858 near the Walker River in western Nevada. He belonged to a tribe that whites call the Northern Paiute. The Cheyenne and Lakota called this tribe "fish-eaters," because their diet included fish from rivers and lakes. In their own language, the Northern Paiute call themselves the Numu, which means "the People."

The traditional life of the Numu was shattered by whites who poured through their lands on the way to the California gold rush in 1849. Ten years later, gold and silver were discovered in Nevada, and the miners cut down the precious piñon pines for their mine shafts and their fires. The Numu depended on the pine nuts for food, especially during the winter. White farmers and ranchers accompanied the miners and claimed the best land for themselves.

In 1860, shortly after Wovoka was born, the Numu fought a series of battles with white miners and soldiers usually called the Pyramid Lake War or Paiute War. Although the Numu won the first battle, the war ended when white soldiers established a fort along the California Trail in Numu territory. While the Indians of the Plains were just beginning to battle the whites, the Numu settled into an uneasy but peaceful coexistence with their white neighbors.

Wovoka's father was a medicine man named Numo-tibo'o, which means "Northern Paiute–White Man." (In some stories of Wovoka, his father's name is Tavibo, which is a simpler spelling of the same name.) Numo-tibo'o probably fought in the Pyramid Lake War and was apparently captured by soldiers and taken away to prison. This might explain the meaning of his name—a Northern Paiute captured by white men. In any event, Numo-tibo'o returned and passed on his knowledge of Numu tradition to his oldest son, Wovoka.

From 1866 to 1872, just as Wovoka was growing toward manhood, the Numu suffered from famine, floods, and white diseases. Three years of drought destroyed their traditional food supplies, which were already threatened by the white intruders. Although some Numu were interested in learning to farm, the government failed to give them the promised support to start a new way of life.

During this hard time, a prophet named Wodziwob appeared on the Walker River Reservation, not far from Wovoka's home in Mason Valley. According to anthropologist Cora Du Bois, "Wodziwob went into a trance, during which he learned that Supreme Ruler . . . was then on his way with all the spirits of the departed dead to again reside upon this earth and change it into a paradise. Life was to be eternal and no distinction was to exist between the races."

Wodziwob instructed the Numu to dance their traditional round dance for five nights in a row. The round dance was a social dance of the Numu, but now it became a dance of spiritual renewal; by dancing, the people welcomed Supreme Ruler and prepared the way for the resurrection of the dead. Wodziwob's spiritual movement is called the 1869 Ghost Dance (or 1870 Ghost Dance) to distinguish it from Wovoka's Ghost Dance 20 years later.

In 1869 Wodziwob prophesied that a train would come from the east carrying Supreme Ruler and all the dead Indians. The first part of this prophecy came true, for that year the transcontinental railroad was completed and trains from the east rolled across Nevada. But Supreme Ruler and the dead Indians did not return.

The Ghost Dance of 1869 died out among the Numu around 1873. The people were disappointed that Wodziwob's prophecies had not come true, and they were disappointed in Wodziwob himself when they discovered him using dynamite to make the earth shake and demonstrate his powers. Also, the lives of the people improved. The pine nut crop of 1873 was the best in years, and the government finally provided some of the promised supplies. For the time being, the Numu forgot the Ghost Dance and concentrated on more earthly concerns.

Wovoka's father, Numo-tibo'o, participated in the Ghost Dance as a follower of Wodziwob. Some stories even call Numo-tibo'o the prophet of the 1869 Ghost Dance, but this is not true. Wovoka was in his early teens during the first Ghost Dance movement, so he probably accompanied his father to the dances and may have participated himself. As he grew toward manhood, he carried with him the knowledge of the first Ghost Dance and the message of Wodziwob.

Wovoka encountered a different spiritual influence from a white family named Wilson who owned a large ranch in Mason Valley. The Wilsons had two sons around his age, and Wovoka and the Wilson boys became playmates. He taught them the Northern Paiute language while they taught him English. As they grew older, Wovoka joined the Wilson brothers in doing chores around the ranch and ate with the family in their big wooden ranch house.

The Wilsons gave Wovoka an English name—Jack Wilson—which he used for the rest of his life in most dealings with whites and Indians alike. Because of this, early historians believed that Wovoka was adopted by the Wilsons after the death of his parents. Actually, Wovoka's parents lived well into the 20th century, and he probably alternated between living with them and living with the Wilson family.

The Wilsons were devout Presbyterians, and Mr. Wilson read from the Bible every morning after breakfast. We don't know how much English Wovoka understood at this time, but he was an intelligent young man who grasped the main ideas in the story of a Messiah and miracle worker named Jesus. It is also possible that he listened to stories of the Old Testament prophets such as Elijah, who brought rain to his people during a terrible drought.

Some older Numu like Numo-tibo'o considered the whites evil intruders, and Numo-tibo'o himself refused to work for the white farmers and ranchers. But Wovoka was of a younger generation raised side by side with whites, and he readily accepted work, not only from the Wilsons, but from other whites of the valley. By the age of 20, Wovoka stood six feet tall and had a powerful, muscular physique. He developed a reputation as an excellent worker, known especially for his ability as a wood-cutter. The name Wovoka means "the Cutter" and was probably given to him as a young man in recognition of this ability. His birth name is unknown.

By the 1880s Wovoka had settled down with a wife and children. His wife's Paiute name was Tumma, but she was known as Mary Wilson. Although he had adopted a white name and supported his family by working for white men, Wovoka was still the son of Numo-tibo'o, a traditional Numu shaman. The Numu believed that at least one son of a shaman inherited his father's power, and it is likely that Numo-tibo'o taught Wovoka many of his secrets.

During the late 1880s, the Numu once again faced a long drought, just as they had in the years before the Ghost Dance of Wodziwob. By this time many Numu had taken up farming, and the drought threatened their crops as well as the crops and ranches of the whites. During this drought, Wovoka began to establish a reputation as a "weather-control doctor." Both Indians and whites recognized his power. Referring to the years from 1886 to 1890, one white settler later recalled, "For five years, [Wovoka] never missed a prophecy concerning weather . . ."

There is evidence that Wovoka reintroduced the Ghost Dance in late 1888 or even earlier, probably as part of his efforts to end the drought. But the turning point came on New Year's Day of 1889. According to one story, Wovoka—the Cutter—was cutting pine trees in the mountains when he suddenly heard a loud noise:

> He laid down his ax and started to go in the direction of the noise, when he fell down dead; and God came and took him to heaven and showed him everything there; it was the most beautiful country you could imagine; he saw both Indians and whites, who were all young; God told him that when the people died here on this earth, if they were good, they come to heaven, and he made them young again, and they never grow to be old afterwards . . .
>
> God came to him again that night and told him to tell all the people that they must not fight, there must be peace all over the world; that the people must not steal from one another, but be good to each other, for they were all brothers, and when he had finished this work God would come after him again.
>
> . . . God had given him great power and authority to do many things; he could cause it to rain and snow at will . . . and God directed him on his return to say to his people that they must meet often and dance five nights in succession and then stop for three months.

According to another story, Wovoka experienced this vision while very ill with scarlet fever. In fact he probably had a number of visions, but his Great Revelation occurred on New Year's Day, 1889, and he recovered during a total solar eclipse. In traditional Numu religion, the sun is the greatest of the powers, and some people may have interpreted Wovoka's miraculous recovery during the eclipse as a sign that he had the power to save the sun.

After his Great Revelation, the news of the Ghost Dance and the new prophet spread outward from Mason Valley—first to the Numu and then to other tribes. That spring Captain Josephus, a Numu leader from the Walker River Reservation, visited Wovoka and asked him to make it rain. Josephus did not believe in Wovoka or the Ghost Dance, but his people were in danger of losing their crops and he was willing to try anything.

Wovoka told Josephus, "You can go home and on the morning of the third day you and all the people will have plenty of water." Josephus went back to the reservation, and shortly afterward it began to rain. On the morning of the third day, he woke up to find the Walker River overflowing its banks, providing the Numu farmers with all the water they needed. From then on, Captain Josephus became "a strong believer in the unnatural powers of the new Christ." It was Captain Josephus who told the story of Wovoka's Great Revelation quoted above.

Along with his power over the weather, Wovoka demonstrated other "unnatural" powers to his followers. He made a block of ice appear from the sky on a hot and cloudless day, and he proved his invulnerability to bullets by having his brother fire a shotgun at him at close range. A white friend of Wovoka named Ed Dyer witnessed both of these events and believed they were tricks that Wovoka had set up beforehand. For instance, Dyer pointed out that a block of ice hidden in a cottonwood tree above Wovoka's head would slip through the branches and fall to the ground as it melted. When a government official later asked Wovoka about the shotgun incident, he replied simply, "That was a joke."

According to people who knew him, Wovoka had a good sense of humor and enjoyed playing practical jokes. But even if some of his "miracles" were tricks to impress his followers, he clearly possessed great spiritual power. His control of the weather was not a joke or a trick. And the message that he preached along with the Ghost Dance was no joke at all.

Wovoka's original teachings combined values from the Judeo-Christian tradition with some uniquely Indian ideas. In January 1892, an anthropologist named James Mooney visited Wovoka in Mason Valley and asked him about his teachings. Mooney's report is very similar to Captain Josephus's description of the teachings a year earlier:

> . . . God told him he must go back and tell his people they must be good and love one another, have no quarreling, and live in peace with the whites; that they must work, and not lie or steal; that they must put away all the old practices that savored of war; that if they faithfully obeyed his instructions they would at last be reunited with their friends in this other world, where there would be no more death or sickness or old age. He was then given the dance which he was commanded to bring back to his people.

Wovoka also told Mooney that God had given him control over the weather and placed him in charge of the West, while President Benjamin Harrison would take care of the East, and God would take care of the world above.

Although Wovoka claimed to be "in charge of the West," there is no evidence that he ever claimed to be the Messiah or the Indian Christ. Nor is there any evidence that he ever preached anything but peace between the whites and Indians. For Wovoka, the Ghost Dance was a sacred ceremony that would prepare his people for eternal happiness in paradise. Thus it was similar to the prayers and ceremonies of all great religions.

Unfortunately Wovoka's peaceful message was changed as it traveled eastward across the Plains. In January 1889, just a few weeks after his Great Revelation, a Ute delegation from Utah arrived in Mason Valley to meet the new prophet. They were the first of a great wave of delegates from over 30 tribes who met Wovoka and returned to their own people to spread the message of the Ghost Dance.

It is not surprising that these apostles came away with different ideas about Wovoka and the meaning of the Ghost Dance.

Wovoka, the Ghost Dance Prophet. The wide-brimmed hat and eagle feather were important symbols of his power. Drawing based on a photograph by anthropologist James Mooney during his visit to Mason Valley, Nevada in January 1892. (National Anthropological Archives, Smithsonian Institution)

Although one delegate reported that Wovoka spoke to each Indian in his own language, in fact he only spoke Northern Paiute and some English. He did not know the sign language that the Plains tribes used to communicate with each other. Thus, most apostles learned his message through translation. But even more significant is the fact that people often believe what they want to believe. In his report on Wovoka, James Mooney told a story that demonstrates this clearly: At the end of their visit, a delegation of Cheyenne and Arapaho asked Wovoka to demonstrate his powers. Wovoka placed his Stetson hat upside down on the ground, made a quick motion with his hand, and apparently pulled something out of the hat. A Cheyenne named Tall Bull said that all he saw was "something black" emerging from the hat—nothing more. But an Arapaho named Black Coyote told Mooney that he had seen "the whole world" in Wovoka's hat. Both men witnessed the same demonstration, but each saw what he wanted to see—an empty hat or the whole world.

In November 1889 a delegation arrived that included two Lakota medicine men, Short Bull and Kicking Bear. When they returned from Nevada the following April, they established the Ghost Dance on the Pine Ridge and Cheyenne River reservations in South Dakota. But the Ghost Dance of Short Bull and Kicking Bear was very different from the Ghost Dance of Wovoka. The Lakota leaders were men of great intelligence and vision in their own right, and they formed the Ghost Dance into a religious movement that satisfied the needs of their own people.

By the time of Wovoka's Great Revelation, the Numu had made peace with the whites and led fairly comfortable lives. Although the drought of the late 1880s threatened the crops of Numu farmers, many Numu men and women worked at various jobs for white bosses in the growing economy of Nevada. In *Wovoka and the Ghost Dance*, anthropologist Michael Hittman writes, "Though their working hours for [whites] were long and wages were marginal, Numus received more food, clothing, and material than ever before seen, and possibly even dreamed."

The Lakota, however, were angry, miserable, and hungry. Once the proudest and most powerful tribe on the Plains, they had been defeated by federal soldiers after years of bitter, bloody warfare. In the summer of 1889, they had been forced to sell half their tribal land to make way for white farmers and ranchers. As part of the

Short Bull. Along with his brother-in-law Kicking Bear, Short Bull developed Wovoka's teachings into the most powerful of the tribal Ghost Dance movements. This photograph was taken by David F. Berry in 1891, when Short Bull and other Lakota Ghost Dancers visited Washington, D.C. while traveling with Buffalo Bill's Wild West show. (National Anthropological Archives, Smithsonian Institution)

land sale, government agents had promised an increase in food rations, but when the treaty was signed the rations were actually decreased.

In this atmosphere of resentment at white domination, the Ghost Dance became more intense, desperate, and warlike than it was among the Numu. Although Wovoka preached peace with the whites, Short Bull prophesied that on a certain date the Messiah would come and drive the whites from the earth, bring the dead Indians with him, and restore the buffalo to the land. As the movement developed, Short Bull may have claimed to be the Messiah himself. Kicking Bear and other Lakota leaders created ghost shirts, which they believed would make the wearers invulnerable to enemy bullets. Wovoka had demonstrated his own invulnerability to bullets, but he denied any knowledge of the ghost shirts.

In October 1890 the Lakota chief Sitting Bull invited his nephew Kicking Bear to conduct the Ghost Dance on the Standing Rock Reservation. Sitting Bull was not a leader of the Ghost Dance, but he strongly defended the traditional Lakota way of life and was sympathetic to the ideals of the dance. The government agent at Standing Rock, James McLaughlin, used the Ghost Dance as an excuse to arrest Sitting Bull. But when Indian policemen tried to arrest him on December 15, 1890, a fight broke out and Sitting Bull was killed, along with seven of his followers and four Indian policemen.

The death of Sitting Bull sent shock waves throughout the Lakota reservations. Fearing that his people would be arrested and sent to prison, a chief named Big Foot led his band—including refugees from Sitting Bull's camp—on a 100-mile flight across the Badlands to the Pine Ridge Reservation, where they were intercepted by federal soldiers. Big Foot's people had never intended to fight, so they peacefully followed the soldiers to a camp near Wounded Knee Creek.

The soldiers surrounded Big Foot's band and pointed four Hotchkiss machine guns at their camp. On the morning of December 29, they ordered the Indians to give up their guns. Big Foot's warriors hid their best weapons, and the soldiers searched the camp. An old medicine man named Yellow Bird stretched his arms

Kicking Bear, a hardened warrior as well as a medicine man. Kicking Bear and Short Bull led the Lakota Ghost Dance movement. In this 1896 photograph by William Dinwiddie, Kicking Bear is wearing his "scalp shirt." (National Anthropological Archives, Smithsonian Institution)

westward toward the coming Messiah and prayed that the people's ghost shirts would keep them safe from the soldiers' bullets.

No one knows exactly how the shooting started or who shot first, but suddenly the camp became a battleground, with rifles blasting and knives flashing. As the Indians rushed past the soldiers, the Hotchkiss guns mowed them down. When it was over, 146 Indians lay dead in the camp near Wounded Knee Creek, including 44 women, 18 children, and Chief Big Foot. Perhaps 30 or 40 others were fatally wounded and staggered away to die elsewhere. Twenty-five soldiers were also killed.

Upon hearing of the massacre, Short Bull, Kicking Bear, and other Ghost Dancers retreated to a secluded area in the Badlands called the Stronghold. Sporadic fighting continued for the next few days, but the Ghost Dancers finally surrendered on January 15, 1891. Short Bull, Kicking Bear, and 23 other Ghost Dance leaders were arrested. The Lakota Ghost Dance was over, and with it died the last hope of Indian freedom from white domination.

A thousand miles away in Mason Valley, Nevada, Wovoka pulled his blanket over his head and mourned when he heard the sad story of Wounded Knee. This was not what he had intended, not what he had seen in his Great Revelation. He had seen a paradise where Indians and whites were forever young and happy, living together in peace. How had this message turned to senseless killing?

After Wounded Knee, Indian delegations continued to visit Wovoka, seeking further knowledge of the Ghost Dance and the coming of the Messiah. Concerned that he might be blamed for the tragedy and frustrated at the way others interpreted his message, Wovoka ordered the delegates to go home and tell their people to stop the dances. Despite his orders, the Ghost Dance continued among some tribes into the 20th century.

Among the Numu, the Ghost Dance movement was centered on the personality and power of Wovoka. When he withdrew into a more private life, the Ghost Dance in the Mason Valley area died out. However, the Numu never lost faith in their prophet, and Wovoka himself never doubted his original message or his spiritual powers. He became a respected shaman credited with many miraculous cures, and he continued to demonstrate his power over the weather. In the late 1890s, Wovoka's only son was killed in a wagon accident. Although unable to bring his son back to life, Wovoka unleashed a mighty rainstorm to cover his tracks on the earth.

Other tribes also retained their faith in Wovoka. Believers wrote him letters asking him to cure sickness in their family or to bring rain to their lands. Usually they included money in the letters and asked for some special object belonging to the Prophet. Wovoka sent them sacred red paint, feathers, an article of his clothing, or one of his black Stetson hats. Wovoka's white friend Ed Dyer helped him with this correspondence, which turned into a profitable mail-order business in spiritual objects.

According to Dyer, Wovoka charged $20.00 for a Stetson hat, $2.50 for an eagle feather, and $1.00 for a magpie feather. This money helped support Wovoka and his family, but it also had a deeper meaning. Like many Indian shamans, Wovoka believed he would lose his power if he did not receive payment for his services. The power had value, and the payment was a fair exchange.

Between 1906 and 1916, Wovoka left his seclusion in Mason Valley to visit followers in Wyoming, Montana, Kansas, and Oklahoma. By this time the hysteria that surrounded Wounded Knee had passed, and he felt safer being out in the open as the Ghost Dance Prophet. He was treated with great respect on these visits and given many valuable gifts. In 1910, during a trip to the Wind River Reservation in Wyoming, the Shoshone held a Ghost Dance in his honor.

In 1919 Wovoka's youngest daughter, Alice Vidovich, gave birth to a son in Carson City, Nevada—about 60 miles from Wovoka's home in Mason Valley. According to the boy's father, Wovoka and his wife Mary arrived at the Vidovich home shortly after the birth, although no one had informed them. On the fourth day of the baby's life, Wovoka performed a traditional ceremony similar to a baptism, praying that the baby would grow up to be healthy in body, mind, and spirit. When the ceremony was over, he made an extraordinary prophecy about his newborn grandson:

> He'll be flying in the skies. And then he's going to join the United States Flying Outfit . . . He'll have a good mind, good body, sharp eyes, everything. And he will lead the white men in the skies. He will become a great captain.

At the time of this prophecy, the airplane was a new invention and there were few planes flying through the skies of Nevada. But Wovoka's grandson, Harlyn Vidovich, did indeed become a commercial airline pilot and fly through the skies. When World War II broke out, he joined the U.S. Air Corps, rose to the rank of captain, and served bravely with the famous Flying Tigers. Vidovich was shot down over China during World War II and given a hero's burial in Nevada.

Wovoka died in Yerrington, Nevada, on September 29, 1932. According to his death certificate, he was 74 years old. Before his death, it was said he made a final prophecy—that if he made it to heaven again he would shake the earth. Three months later, the Mason Valley shook with the most powerful earthquake that most residents had ever felt in their lives. To Numu believers this was the final proof of their prophet's greatness. Even white nonbelievers were impressed. A former county sheriff exclaimed, "Son-of-a-gun, Jack! Said he was gonna shake this world if he made it [to heaven], and, by God, he did!"

In the end, it doesn't really matter whether Wovoka shook the earth. Nor does it matter whether he could control the weather or make a block of ice appear from the sky. What matters is the message of his Great Revelation. On his tombstone, the following words sum up the importance of Wovoka's life:

Wovoka, 1858–1932
Founder of the Ghost Dance
His teachings of hope, good will, and promise of life after death
will live as long as man inhabits the earth

BLACK ELK

◆ ◆ ◆

Lakota Holy Man

During the American Civil War, the Lakota still lived the old way on the western Plains. They followed the buffalo, battled their traditional enemies, and worshiped Wakan Tanka, the Great Mysterious. In the winter, after the last buffalo hunt, the Lakota bands each camped beside one of the many rivers that cut through the Plains. As the snow and wind whipped across the barren landscape, they stayed warm in their lodges, eating dried buffalo meat and wrapping themselves in buffalo robes before the fire.

In December 1863, a Lakota baby was born at a winter camp along the Powder River in what is now Wyoming. His parents called him Chance, but when later given a man's name, he would be called Black Elk—the name of his father, his grandfather, and his great-grandfather. The older Black Elks were respected medicine men among the Lakota. And this baby, the young Black Elk, was destined to be a medicine man as well.

The Lakota, also called the Teton Sioux, were one of the largest and strongest tribes in North America. In 1850, before the whites destroyed their traditional way of life, there were about 15,000 Lakota divided into seven subtribes. Black Elk belonged to the largest subtribe, the Oglala. When Black Elk was born, the Oglala ranged across the western Plains in what is now Nebraska, Colorado, Wyoming, and Montana. But even as he took his first breath, the old way of the Lakota was threatened by the whites.

In 1868 the Lakota and the U.S. government signed a treaty

establishing the Great Sioux Reservation in what is now the Dakotas. Many Oglala moved onto the reservation, but others—including Black Elk's family—chose to stay on the open Plains, following
the buffalo and leading the traditional life of their people. The
leader of the free Oglala was Crazy Horse, a distant relative of
Black Elk's father. Black Elk called him his cousin.

Around this time, when he was five years old, Black Elk had his
first vision. His father had just made him his first bow and arrow,
and he set out into the woods, hoping to find a small bird to shoot.
But just as he stepped among the trees, he saw a thunderstorm
coming and heard a voice calling him. As an old man, he described
this first mystical experience:

> I saw two men coming out of a cloud with spears. As I was looking
> up to that, there was a kingbird sitting there and these two men
> were coming toward me singing the sacred song and that bird told
> me to listen to the two men. The kingbird said: "Look, the clouds
> all over are one-sided, a voice is calling you." I looked up and the
> two men were coming down singing:
> Behold him, a sacred voice is calling you.
> All over the sky a sacred voice is calling you.
> I stood gazing at them and they were coming from the north; they
> started toward the west and [turned into] geese.

After this first vision, Black Elk always felt that someone was
calling him. But this was only a small taste of the mystical experience that awaited him. Four years later, when he was nine years
old, Black Elk fell off his horse and crumpled to the ground. He
grew very ill and lay in his family's tipi for 12 days. During that
time, Black Elk experienced one of the greatest visions ever recorded in spiritual literature.

As he told it years later, Black Elk's vision was long and com-
plicated, with many wonderful details of the spirit world. We
cannot consider all of these details, but to understand the life of
Black Elk we must understand the main images of his vision.

While he lay in his tipi, the two men from his first vision
descended from the clouds and said, "Hurry up, your grandfather
is calling you." Black Elk rose and followed them back up into the
sky, riding on his own small cloud. The men showed him a bay

horse standing in the middle of the clouds. "Behold me," said the horse, "my life history you shall see."

The bay horse showed Black Elk the horses of the four directions: 12 black horses of the west, 12 white horses of the north, 12 sorrel horses of the east, and 12 buckskin horses of the south. The horses lined up in formation and suddenly millions of other horses filled the sky. Then the horses turned into buffalo, elk, and other animals and returned to the four directions.

Now the bay horse led Black Elk to the tipi of the six grandfathers—spirit beings who represented the four directions, the sky, and the earth. The tipi rested on a cloud beneath a rainbow gate. Each of the first four grandfathers gave Black Elk something to help him in his mission on the earth.

The grandfather of the west gave him a wooden cup filled with water. "Take courage and be not afraid . . . you shall be very powerful on earth in medicines and all powers." The grandfather of the north gave him a sacred, healing herb. "Behold the mother earth, for you shall create a nation." The grandfather of the east gave him a peace pipe with a spotted eagle on the handle. "Behold this, for with this you shall walk across the earth . . . whatever is sick on this earth you shall make well."

The grandfather of the south gave him a stick. "Behold this, with this to the nation's center of the earth, many you shall save." Before Black Elk's astonished eyes, the stick began to grow and flower like a plant. Then the fourth grandfather showed him two roads: the good red road from north to south and the hard black road of fearfulness from east to west.

The fifth grandfather, who represented the Great Spirit above, said, "Boy, I sent for you and you came. Behold me, my power you shall see." Then he turned into a spotted eagle and said, "Things in the sky shall be like relatives. They shall take you across the earth with my power. Your grandfathers shall attack an enemy and be unable to destroy him, but you shall have the power to destroy. You shall go with courage."

Finally the sixth grandfather, who represented the earth, said, "Boy, take courage, you wanted my power on earth, so you shall know me. You shall have my power in going back to the earth.

Your nation on earth shall have great difficulties. There you shall go. Behold me, for I will depart."

Black Elk followed the sixth grandfather out of the cloud tipi and through the rainbow gate. As he studied the white-haired grandfather more closely, it seemed that he recognized him. Suddenly the grandfather began to change, growing younger and younger until he became a nine-year-old boy. Then Black Elk realized that he himself was the sixth grandfather—the representative of Wakan Tanka on the earth.

This was only the beginning of Black Elk's great vision. After leaving the cloud tipi of the grandfathers, he walked the black road of fearfulness and destroyed an evil monster that rose from the waters of the Missouri River. Then he walked the good red road and received the sacred hoop of the Lakota nation. The Lakota people rejoiced as the flowering stick was planted in the center of the sacred hoop.

As his vision continued, Black Elk received a second healing herb and witnessed the horse dance, "more beautiful than anything could be." When the dance was over, he traveled to the center of the earth and received the daybreak star herb. "Behold this," said the spirits, "with this on earth you shall undertake anything and accomplish it." Then Black Elk saw a vision of war and received the soldier weed, the most powerful herb of all, for it could destroy a nation. "There will be disputes of nations," the spirits told him, "and you will defend your people with this herb."

Finally Black Elk returned to the cloud tipi of the grandfathers. The sixth grandfather showed him a cup of water containing the Lakota and their brothers, the Cheyenne. "Behold them, this is your nation and you shall go back to them . . . Now in a sacred manner you shall walk." A spotted eagle guided Black Elk back to earth. When he woke up, he was in his own tipi with his parents bending over him. His vision had cured him of the sickness.

For the next eight years, Black Elk tried to forget about his vision. He told no one, because he feared the great responsibility that the grandfathers had given him—to save the Lakota people and make the stick bloom within the sacred hoop. During this period Black Elk tried to live the life of a Lakota boy: playing games, riding ponies, and hunting with his friends. But the power of his vision would not go away.

The two men who had descended from the sky to guide him were Thunder-beings, and he could always tell when a thunderstorm was approaching. He had other mystical feelings too. When he was 12, he witnessed the defeat of Custer's army at the Little Bighorn. As the battle raged around him he remembered his vision and later said, "I knew that we were going to wipe out the soldiers." Although too young to participate as a warrior, Black Elk scalped an injured soldier and killed him with a six-shooter.

A year after the battle, the great Oglala leader Crazy Horse was murdered by some of his own people at Fort Robinson, Nebraska. Many of Crazy Horse's followers, including Black Elk's family, fled north to join Sitting Bull in Canada. There Black Elk continued to fight the power and responsibility of his great vision, but he could not ignore it. One winter, when his people faced starvation, he went hunting with his father and understood the howl of a coyote telling him where to find the buffalo.

In the spring of 1880, Black Elk's people returned to the United States and camped at Fort Keogh in Montana. That June they held a sun dance, the great ritual ceremony of the Lakota. During the dance the full power of his vision came back to Black Elk. From then on he heard voices all the time, and he was terrified of the Thunder-beings whenever storm clouds rolled in from the west.

Finally that winter Black Elk revealed part of his vision to an old medicine man, who was amazed by the greatness of the young boy's vision. In Lakota belief, one who is blessed with a great vision should perform it on earth for the benefit of his people. The old medicine man told Black Elk that this was his first duty.

In the spring of 1881, Black Elk performed the horse dance from his vision. Black Elk himself rode on a bay horse like the one that had guided him through the clouds, while others rode the horses of the four directions. There was a tipi with a rainbow painted over the door and two roads drawn across the floor. Six old men represented the six grandfathers, and four young girls carried the healing herb of the north, the spotted eagle pipe, the flowering stick, and the sacred hoop of the nation.

The performance of the horse dance was a great success for Black Elk and for his people. Later he described his new feelings after the dance:

> After the ceremony was completed, it seemed that I was above the earth and I did not touch the earth. I felt very happy and I was also happy to see my people, as it looked like they were renewed and happy. They all greeted me and were very generous to me, telling me that their relatives here and there were sick and were cured in a mysterious way . . . I was now recognized as a medicine man at the age of seventeen.

After the horse dance, Black Elk moved to Pine Ridge on the Sioux Reservation in South Dakota, where most of the Oglala lived. The following spring he went on a traditional vision quest, with a ritual sweat bath followed by fasting in the wilderness. Once again Wakan Tanka blessed him with a vision of Thunder-beings. Black Elk performed part of this vision in a *heyoka* ceremony, in which he and other thunder-dreamers acted like clowns, doing everything backward to make the spectators laugh. Later Black Elk repeated the horse dance for the people of Pine Ridge, so that they would understand the power of his original vision.

If he had been born in an earlier time, Black Elk probably would have spent his life following the traditional path of a Lakota medicine man. But the old life of the Lakota was slowly dying on the reservation. Black Elk realized that the whites were now the rulers of the land, and he wanted to learn more about the white world. In 1886 he joined Buffalo Bill's Wild West show as a dancer, traveling first to New York and then to England, where he performed before Queen Victoria.

When the show returned to the United States in the spring of 1888, Black Elk and two other Indians became separated from the rest of the troupe. They joined another Wild West show and toured through Germany, France, and Italy. During his travels, Black Elk learned some English and began to study Christianity. In a letter to a Lakota newspaper, he wrote:

. . . of the white man's many customs, only his faith, the white
man's beliefs about God's will, and how they act according to it, I
wanted to understand . . . So Lakota people, trust in God! Now all
along I trust in God . . . Across the big ocean is where they killed
Jesus; again I wished to see it but it was four days on the ocean and
there was no railroad . . . [It would require] much money for me to
be able to go over there to tell about it myself.

Black Elk's desire to see the Holy Land in order to "tell about it
myself" is typical of the Lakota attitude toward religion. Lakota
religion was not based on faith or books. It was based on direct
experience of Wakan Tanka—the kind of experience Black Elk had
gained in his great vision.

When he returned to Pine Ridge in the fall of 1889, Black Elk found
his people suffering from hunger and despair. That summer government authorities had forced the Sioux to sell half their land to make
room for white farmers and ranchers. The remaining land was
divided into six smaller reservations, including Pine Ridge. Although the government had promised more food as part of the land
sale, they actually cut food rations once the agreement was signed.

Faced with starvation and misery, the Lakota eagerly embraced
the Ghost Dance, a powerful religious movement that swept across
the Plains in 1890. The Ghost Dance began with the visions of a
Northern Paiute Indian named Wovoka, who taught that the
dance would lead to a heavenly paradise where Indians and
whites could live together in peace.

During the winter of 1889–90, two Lakota religious leaders,
Short Bull and Kicking Bear, visited Wovoka in Nevada and
returned with their own version of the Ghost Dance, designed to
ease the frustration of the Lakota people. The Lakota leaders
preached that the dance would prepare the way for an Indian
Messiah, who would drive the whites from the land and establish
an earthly paradise where the dead Indians would live again and
the herds of buffalo would once again thunder over the Plains. (For
more information on the Ghost Dance, see the profile of Wovoka
on page 80.)

At first Black Elk was skeptical of the new religion, but when he
went to see the Ghost Dance for himself he felt as if he had been

struck by lightning. The Lakota Ghost Dancers moved in a sacred circle around a great tree—just like the flowering tree within the sacred hoop of his vision. Black Elk joined the Ghost Dance, and after two days of dancing he fell to the ground with a new vision. He later said that he designed the famous Lakota ghost shirts based on shirts he saw in this vision. Actually a number of leaders—including Black Elk and Kicking Bear—designed ghost shirts, which were believed to make the wearer invulnerable to enemy bullets.

The Lakota Ghost Dance movement was crushed in December 1890, when federal soldiers killed over 150 men, women, and children at Wounded Knee. Black Elk heard the shooting and led a group of warriors in a heroic attempt to save his people. He charged untouched through the soldiers' bullets, his ghost shirt and sacred bow protecting him. But though Black Elk and his warriors saved some Lakota who had been captured by the soldiers, they could not prevent the massacre. Bloody corpses lay scattered on the hard ground and dying moans echoed through the air.

The Ghost Dance was over. And to Black Elk, the end of the Ghost Dance marked the end of his dream for the Lakota nation to flower again within the sacred hoop.

Despite his bitter disappointment, Black Elk continued practicing traditional healing and religious ceremonies, gaining fame and respect among his people. In 1892 he married Katie War Bonnet and they had three sons. Katie was probably a Catholic, and all three children were baptized in the Catholic Church, which maintained a strong missionary program among the Lakota. However, Black Elk still held to the old ways. Then in 1904, a year after Katie's death, Black Elk embarked on a new path.

According to his daughter—who was not yet born at the time—Black Elk was performing a traditional healing ceremony over a dying boy when a Catholic priest stormed into the tipi, ripped the sacred objects from his hands and shouted, "Satan, get out!" Black Elk felt that the priest's power was greater than his own, so he left the tipi and sat outside while the priest performed the last rites of the Catholic Church over the boy.

When the priest had finished, he invited Black Elk to return with him to the mission.

On December 6, 1904, Black Elk was baptized into the Catholic Church as Nicholas Black Elk. He gave up the sacred healing rites and dances of the Lakota religion. The former medicine man joined the Catholic men's organization and later became an instructor who taught other Indians about the Catholic Church. He was such an effective teacher that the church sent him as a missionary to other tribes. According to one estimate, Black Elk was personally responsible for converting over 400 Indians to Roman Catholicism.

In 1906, two years after his conversion, Black Elk married a widow named Annie Brings White. Annie had a young daughter of her own, and she and Black Elk had a daughter and a son. Annie was also active in the Catholic Church, and the two of them became respected leaders of the Catholic Lakota on the Pine Ridge Reservation. In 1926 a Catholic missionary built a house for Black Elk next to the church. When the priest couldn't come, Black Elk led services for the congregation.

It is difficult to completely understand Black Elk's conversion from Lakota medicine man to Catholic teacher. His daughter's story may be true, but there were other reasons as well. In his great vision, Black Elk had received the soldier weed with the power to destroy the enemies of his people. According to his vision, he was supposed to use this powerful weapon in 1900. But when the time came, Black Elk did not have the heart to unleash destruction on the whites, fearing he might kill innocent women and children. It is possible that he believed he had lost the power of his vision by refusing to use the soldier weed.

Another explanation is that Black Elk joined the Catholic Church in order to continue his role as a spiritual leader of the Lakota community while adapting to a world controlled by the whites. Black Elk himself rarely discussed his conversion. When a white friend asked him why he had given up his old religion, he replied simply, "My children had to live in this world."

Outwardly, Black Elk lived a good Catholic life on the Pine Ridge Reservation. To the missionaries he represented one of their greatest success stories—a traditional Lakota medicine man who had completely accepted the Catholic religion. But in Black Elk's heart the power of his original vision still burned.

In August 1930 a white man named John G. Neihardt came to visit Black Elk. Neihardt—the poet laureate of Nebraska—was working on an epic poem about the Ghost Dance and Wounded Knee, and he wanted to talk to Black Elk about those times. But he learned much more than he had expected.

Black Elk sensed that John Neihardt was a special person who was sent to him for a special purpose. He said, "As I sit here, I can feel in this man beside me a strong desire to know the things of the Other World. He has been sent to learn what I know, and I will teach him."

The following spring Neihardt returned to Black Elk's house, and they began a series of sessions in which Black Elk told Neihardt the story of his life, including the great vision. Black Elk adopted Neihardt as his son, naming him Flaming Rainbow in honor of the rainbow over the cloud tipi in his vision. In *The Sixth Grandfather*, anthropologist Raymond DeMallie describes the powerful connection between Black Elk and John Neihardt:

> It was as if something long bound up inside the old man had broken free at last, an impulse to save the entire system of knowledge that his vision represented, and that for more than twenty-five years he had denied. Since becoming a Catholic, Black Elk had strictly put away the old ceremonies and his healing rituals. He had accepted the white man's religion and the white man's ways, and this would not change. But the vision, and his failure to live up to it, must have been a heavy burden. This burden he could at long last transfer to another man—someone who could record the old Lakota ways as testament and memorial to a way of life now gone forever.

The story of Black Elk's life and his great vision was published in 1932 as *Black Elk Speaks*. Although the book reflected the essence of Black Elk's words, John G. Neihardt used his own great talents to turn the story into a beautiful, tragic tale of the lost life-way of the Lakota. When it was first published, *Black Elk Speaks* was praised by critics and scholars, but it sold few copies and soon disappeared from the bookstores. During the

Depression people had little money for books.

On the Pine Ridge Reservation, the book caused a stir among the Catholic missionaries, who were disturbed that their prize pupil had secretly held on to his "pagan" beliefs. The missionaries probably pressured Black Elk to reaffirm his belief in the Catholic Church. In a document entitled "Black Elk Speaks Again—The Final Speech," he did so in very clear terms:

> I shake hands with my white friends. Listen! I will speak words of truth. I told about the people's ways of long [ago] and some of this a white man put in a book but he did not tell about current ways . . . For the last thirty years I have lived very differently from what the white man told about me. I am a believer . . . I have converted and live in the true faith of God the Father, the Son, and the Holy Spirit.

Despite his "confession," Black Elk remained close to John Neihardt, and his experience with the poet seemed to waken the old ways within him. He joined again in Lakota dances, and for many summers he starred in a pageant for tourists in the Black Hills of South Dakota. Black Elk played the role of a Lakota medicine man and performed various Lakota rituals, including a traditional healing ceremony. For Black Elk, the pageant was another opportunity to preserve the old traditions of the Lakota.

In 1944 John Neihardt returned to Pine Ridge and interviewed Black Elk and another old Oglala man about the history of the Lakota before the coming of the whites. Neihardt retold these stories in *When the Tree Flowered,* published in 1951. Black Elk also worked with a young scholar named Joseph Epes Brown to preserve the seven sacred rituals of the Oglala. His account of these rituals was published in 1953 as *The Sacred Pipe.*

Black Elk died at Manderson, South Dakota, on August 19, 1950. He was 86 years old. Before he died he received Holy Communion and Extreme Unction, the last rites of the Catholic Church—the religion he had followed faithfully for more than half of his long life.

Eleven years later, in 1961, *Black Elk Speaks* was republished. Now the time was right, and the book became a great success. A new generation of young people, both Indian and white, were

Black Elk in 1947, holding his sacred pipe. Photograph by Joseph Epes Brown.
(National Anthropological Archives, Smithsonian Institution)

fascinated with this story of a time when people loved the land, followed the buffalo, and searched for visions of Wakan Tanka, the Great Mysterious.

To the end of his life, Black Elk believed that he had failed in carrying out the responsibility of his great vision—to make the tree bloom and bring his people back into the sacred hoop. But through the success of *Black Elk Speaks*, the vision of a nine-year-old Lakota boy continues to live today. And in a small way, perhaps, the tree blooms once again in the sacred hoop of the Lakota Nation.

MOUNTAIN WOLF WOMAN

◆ ◆ ◆

Winnebago Seeker and Visionary

In April 1884 a Winnebago girl was born in western Wisconsin. Traditionally, the Winnebago call each child by a birth name that tells its sex and birth order. This baby girl was the youngest of eight children and the fifth daughter, so she was called by a birth name meaning "Fifth Daughter."

Later she would receive a formal clan name, taken from the names passed down in one of the 12 Winnebago clans. Usually the formal name came from the father's clan, but sometimes a child might receive a name from another clan. Such a child was doubly blessed, for she was then protected by two clans—the clan of her father and the clan of her name. Fifth Daughter was destined for this good fortune.

When she was two years old, Fifth Daughter became deathly ill. Her mother sent for an old lady named Wolf Woman who had a reputation as a healer. "I want my little girl to live," she told Wolf Woman. "I give her to you. Whatever way you can make her live, she will be yours." Her mother did not actually give Fifth Daughter up to live with the old woman; she offered her as a symbolic gift, the highest gift possible.

Wolf Woman was so honored by this gift that she began to cry. "You have made me think of myself," she said. "You gave me this dear little child . . . Let it be thus. My life, let her use it. My grandchild, let her use my existence. I will give my name to my own child. The name that I am going to give her is a holy name. She will reach an old age."

Many years later—when she did indeed reach an old age—Fifth Daughter told this story and said, "There they named me with a Wolf Clan name . . . It means to make a home in a bluff or a mountain, as the wolf does, but in English I just say my name is Mountain Wolf Woman."

Mountain Wolf Woman grew up during a period of transition for her people. Like other tribes east of the Mississippi River, the Winnebago had been forced to give up their traditional homeland during the first half of the 19th century. The southern bands signed treaties in 1829 and 1832, trading their land in Wisconsin and northern Illinois for a promised homeland west of the Mississippi. For over 30 years, they were shuffled from reservation to reservation in the West, suffering bitterly from hunger and disease. Finally, in 1865, they settled on a reservation in northeastern Nebraska.

During this period, the northern Winnebago bands resisted removal. Although some leaders signed a treaty in 1837, many of the northern Winnebago believed that the land sale was illegal. They hid from government troops and struggled to continue their traditional life in central and western Wisconsin. Sometimes they were captured by the soldiers and sent to whatever western reservation the other Winnebago were currently living on. But they returned again and again to their Wisconsin homeland. Finally, after the last removal in 1874, the government gave up trying to force the Winnebago from Wisconsin and allowed them to claim homesteads on public land.

Mountain Wolf Woman's family returned to Wisconsin from Nebraska sometime before she was born. Her father would not claim a homestead because he was a member of the Thunder Clan. "I do not belong to the earth," he said. "I have no concern with land." In traditional Winnebago society, only the Bear Clan was concerned with land.

Mountain Wolf Woman's mother was a member of the Eagle Clan, but she decided to claim a homestead near Black River Falls in western Wisconsin. "By this means we will have someplace to live," she said. Despite his refusal to claim the land, her father built them a fine log house on their homestead.

The family was happy to be back in Wisconsin, and they resumed their traditional existence: hunting, trapping, fishing, planting corn and other vegetables, gathering wild berries and other plant foods. But much had changed since the government had tried to force the Winnebago across the Mississippi River. Now they were surrounded by white people, and they had to adapt to the white man's world. When they picked berries or trapped muskrats or wove baskets, they sold them to the whites for money.

Of course, money was not all that the whites had brought to Wisconsin. They had also brought their schools, their language, and their religion. When she was nine years old, one of Mountain Wolf Woman's older brothers announced, "My little sister should go to school. I like to hear women speak English." For the next two years she attended a government boarding school for Indian children at Tomah, Wisconsin.

After her first experience with white education, Mountain Wolf Woman returned to her family. That winter they visited her grandfather on the East Fork of the Black River—the place where she was born. There her mother instructed her in the traditional Winnebago beliefs about a girl's first menstrual period:

> Some time that is going to happen to you. From about the age of thirteen years this happens to girls. When that happens to you, run to the woods and hide some place. You should not look at any one, not even a glance. If you look at a man you will contaminate his blood. Even a glance will cause you to be an evil person. When women are in that condition they are unclean.

One morning after this lesson, Mountain Wolf Woman woke up with the condition her mother described. She ran into the snowy woods, covered her head with a blanket, and began to cry. Suddenly she heard the voices of her older sister and sister-in-law. They built a small wigwam for her and made a fire in the middle. There she fasted for four days and nights. On the third night she dreamed of a wide meadow filled with horses of all colors. When she recalled this dream later, she considered it a prophecy, for she received many horses as gifts during her life.

The following year Mountain Wolf Woman's family moved to Wittenberg in central Wisconsin, near her father's relatives. There she attended a Lutheran mission school for several years and was baptized a Christian. During this period her older brothers went on tour with an Indian dance troupe and sent her a bicycle. "Oh, I was proud," she remembered. "I was the first to have a bicycle, a girl's bicycle. My brothers did that for me."

Although her brothers showed their love by sending the bicycle, they also exercised traditional control over her life. Mountain Wolf Woman's education ended abruptly in her mid-teens, when she was removed from school and informed that she was about to be married. The marriage had been arranged by an older brother who fell asleep after getting drunk and discovered the would-be suitor fanning flies from his face. Then and there he decided that his youngest sister should marry the man. His brothers agreed.

Mountain Wolf Woman cried and begged her mother for help, but it was no use. To refuse the marriage would disgrace her brothers. Even worse, it would break a tribal taboo and possibly cause them great harm. The marriage was sealed by a ritual gift exchange. Dressed in her finest clothing and jewelry, Mountain Wolf Woman rode her pony to the home of her new husband. There she gave away her clothing and jewelry to his female relatives. In return they gave her more clothing and jewelry, and six horses.

After her first daughter was born, Mountain Wolf Woman was initiated into the medicine lodge by her husband's family. The medicine lodge was a traditional religious society dedicated to health and long life for its members. Its ceremonies included moral teachings, tribal history, songs, dances, feasts, herbal knowledge, and mysterious rituals. As part of the initiation ceremony, each new member received a medicine bag containing sacred items of power. Mountain Wolf Woman's mother-in-law promised her a special otterskin medicine bag, but when the time came she gave her a less desirable medicine bag instead.

To Mountain Wolf Woman this symbolized the poor way she was treated by her husband's family. But even worse was the jealous behavior of her husband, who constantly accused her of being unfaithful. After her second daughter was born, Mountain Wolf Woman and her husband went to Black River Falls for a tribal gathering called a powwow. When the powwow ended, she told her husband to go back to Wittenberg alone. She and her two children would stay with her own family at Black River Falls.

That fall and winter, Mountain Wolf Woman participated in traditional medicine dances and helped initiate another woman into the medicine lodge. She was happy as a single mother, but people began to talk about her and a man named Bad Soldier. Although the rumors were not true, Bad Soldier sent her letters. Her oldest brother encouraged her to marry again so that he could visit her; it was not proper for a brother to visit an unmarried sister.

Mountain Wolf Woman did not want to marry Bad Soldier, but she took her oldest brother's request seriously. It was more reasonable than her other brother's promising her to a man who swept flies from his face. Bad Soldier had no family to provide a traditional gift exchange, so they were married under the white man's law at the county courthouse. Despite her doubts, Mountain Wolf Woman and Bad Soldier shared a long, happy marriage.

Around the time of her second marriage, Mountain Wolf Woman's parents and most of her brothers and sisters moved to the Winnebago Reservation in Nebraska. When she became pregnant with her third child, Mountain Wolf Woman followed them and went to live with an older sister, who suggested a different approach to childbirth: "Little sister, when people are in that condition they use peyote. They have children without much suffering. Perhaps you can do that. You always suffer so much. This way you will have it easily."

Peyote is a small spineless cactus that grows in Mexico and Texas. Eating the top of the cactus, called a peyote button, produces visions and an overall feeling of strength and well-being. In the area where peyote grows, Indians have used it for medicinal and religious purposes for thousands of years. But it was only during the 19th century that peyote spread northward to the tribes of the Plains. By the time Mountain Wolf Woman first used peyote in the early 20th century, many tribes—including the Winnebago—used peyote in religious ceremonies and childbirth.

Mountain Wolf Woman did as her sister suggested and gave birth to a boy. Although her first use of the drug was medicinal, this was the beginning of her conversion to the peyote religion. Her husband and family also converted. As she later remembered, "From that time on whenever they held peyote meetings we all attended."

There are two main types of ceremonies in the peyote religion: the Half Moon and the Cross Fire. Both ceremonies combine Indian and Christian beliefs. However, the Half Moon ceremony places more emphasis on traditional ideas such as the Great Spirit and the ritual use of tobacco, while the Cross Fire ceremony uses more Christian ideas, including baptism and readings from the Bible. The Winnebago adopted the Cross Fire ceremony.

When Mountain Wolf Woman first attended peyote meetings she was very shy, sitting quietly with her head bowed, afraid that people would look at her. Then one night she had an extraordinary vision. First she saw a great storm approaching, with whirling black clouds, raging winds, and earthquakes. People were running ahead of the storm, carrying bundles on their backs, desperately trying to escape the destruction.

> . . . I thought to myself, "Where are they fleeing? Nowhere on this earth is there any place to run to. There is not any place for life. Where are they saying they are fleeing to? Jesus is the only place to flee to." This is what I thought.
>
> Then I saw Jesus standing there. I saw that he had one hand raised high. The right hand, high in the air . . . Whatever he was doing, I was to do also . . . I stood up and raised my arm. I prayed. I asked for a good life, thanking God who gave me life . . . There was a sensation of great joyousness. Now I was an angel. That is how I saw myself. Because I had wings I was supposed to fly but I could not quite get my feet off the ground. I wanted to fly right away, but I could not because my time is not yet completed.

After her vision of Jesus, Mountain Wolf Woman became a true believer in the peyote religion. "I knew when I ate peyote that they were using something holy," she said. "That way is directed toward God."

Bad Soldier and Mountain Wolf Woman stayed in Nebraska and ran a farm for several years. When they tired of farming, they moved to the Pine Ridge Sioux Reservation in South Dakota, where they continued to participate in peyote ceremonies and Mountain Wolf Woman was formally adopted by a Sioux family. Finally, after returning briefly to Nebraska, they decided to go back to their traditional homeland in Wisconsin. By this time Mountain Wolf Woman and Bad Soldier had a growing family, so they left the daughters from her first marriage with her older sister, who had no children of her own.

Shortly before their return to Wisconsin, Mountain Wolf Woman's brother—known by the English name Sam Blowsnake—became a peyote "roadman," a leader who knew the peyote songs and could hold ceremonies. It was Sam who had arranged her first marriage to a man who helped him when he was drunk, but he had given up drinking since his conversion to the peyote religion.

In 1908 Sam Blowsnake, Mountain Wolf Woman, Bad Soldier, and other peyotists returned to Black River Falls. They were the first followers of the peyote religion in Wisconsin, and more traditional Winnebagos opposed them bitterly. A white man invited them to settle on his land and hold their meetings. That fall about 100 visitors from Nebraska arrived for a big peyote meeting that lasted for two days and two nights.

The peyote religion was not only opposed by traditional Indians; it was also opposed by the white authorities. In 1918 peyotists in Oklahoma organized the Native American Church to protect their religious rights. Three years later the Nebraska Winnebago organized the Peyote Church of Christ. Peyote churches were later organized in other states, including Wisconsin.

In 1920 Sam Blowsnake wrote about his conversion to the peyote religion in *Autobiography of a Winnebago Indian*, edited by anthropologist Paul Radin. A longer version of the story was later published in which Sam Blowsnake was called Crashing Thunder; however, this was actually the clan name of his oldest brother (known in English as Jasper Blowsnake), who had told

Radin about his own life in an earlier, short autobiography. Sam Blowsnake's story was one of the first full-length autobiographies of an American Indian, and it gained great attention among scholars.

While her brother's story became famous, Mountain Wolf Woman continued to practice the peyote religion in Wisconsin. At the same time, she belonged to a Christian church at Black River Falls, where her children attended the mission school and were baptized. She also participated in traditional Winnebago dances and learned the secrets of Indian medicines from her brother-in-law. Mountain Wolf Woman saw no conflict among the peyote religion, Christianity, and traditional Winnebago beliefs. They were all part of her identity as a Winnebago woman.

From her two marriages, Mountain Wolf Woman had 11 children, eight of whom lived to adulthood. After her own unhappy experience in an arranged marriage, she insisted that her children be free to marry whomever they chose. But when a daughter's marriage fell apart, she exercised the traditional Winnebago right to "claim" her grandchildren, and she raised them herself. This was just one example of how Mountain Wolf Woman tried to keep what was good from the old ways while accepting new ideas.

After Bad Soldier's death in 1936, Mountain Wolf Woman had a new house built near the mission and lived there for the rest of her life as a respected leader of the Winnebago community. Although she considered the peyote religion her true spiritual path, she occasionally participated in traditional Winnebago ceremonies out of respect for her family. In 1945 she attended a Victory Dance to honor the Winnebago soldiers who had fought in World War II. The Victory Dance was one of the oldest Winnebago war ceremonies, and a returning Winnebago soldier brought the scalp of a dead German soldier to use during the dance.

Although she was over 60 years old, Mountain Wolf Woman danced all night for two nights, which was the old way of her people. The more traditional Winnebago did not approve of the peyote religion, but she noticed that only the "peyote people" danced the Victory Dance the old way, never stopping during the

Mountain Wolf Woman. Before publication of Mountain Wolf Woman's autobiography, Nancy Lurie took her to photographer James Speltz in Black River Falls for this formal sitting. (Courtesy Nancy Oestreich Lurie and Paulette Molin.)

two nights. When she returned from the dance, Mountain Wolf Woman lay down to rest and had a vision of the dead German soldier, his blond hair in a wavy pompadour. "We beat you," she said in her vision.

Around the time of the Victory Dance, Mountain Wolf Woman met a young anthropologist named Nancy Lurie, who was studying Winnebago culture. Lurie had been formally adopted by a cousin of Mountain Wolf Woman named Mitchell Redcloud, Sr. According to Winnebago tradition, this made Nancy Lurie the niece of Mountain Wolf Woman. When her niece asked her to tell the story of her life, she could not refuse.

It took 13 years for the idea to become a reality. Finally in January 1958, Mountain Wolf Woman flew to Ann Arbor, Michigan in her first ride on an airplane. For five weeks she worked with Lurie, telling the story of her life into a tape recorder—first in Winnebago, then in English. The story was published in 1961 as *Mountain Wolf Woman, Sister of Crashing Thunder: The Autobiography of a Winnebago Indian.*

Mountain Wolf Woman died at Black River Falls on the morning of November 9, 1960. According to one relative, she predicted the day of her death—a power that the Winnebago believe is given to those who are good, wise, and old. Her funeral reflected the three religions that she embraced during her life. Some relatives held a traditional Winnebago wake, while others held a peyote meeting at her house. Finally she was buried in the mission cemetery after a Christian funeral service.

Mountain Wolf Woman was not a spiritual leader in the same way that the Shawnee Prophet or Wovoka were leaders. She did not start a new religion or lead a great spiritual revival. But she played a leading role in bringing the peyote religion to Wisconsin. And she showed how a traditional Indian woman might live in a white-dominated world, not only by combining religious beliefs, but also by combining different ways of living.

Mountain Wolf Woman's intelligence, good sense, and good nature helped her walk this difficult path between Indian tradition and the modern world. One reviewer called her story "the record of a great old lady recalling a momentous life."

RUBY MODESTO

◆ ◆ ◆

Desert Cahuilla Medicine Woman

Today the Coachella Valley of Southern California is famous for desert resorts like Palm Springs and Indian Wells. Hotels, houses, shops, restaurants, swimming pools, and golf courses cover the land. During the winter, tourists escape the harsh northern winters and come to bask in the warm desert sun. When the sun grows too hot, they ride an aerial tram up Mount San Jacinto, its majestic, snow-capped peak rising more than 10,000 feet above the valley floor.

One hundred and fifty years ago, a very different life existed in the valley—the life of the Desert Cahuilla Indians. The Cahuilla lived in small villages throughout the valley. Although many whites view the desert as a harsh environment, the Cahuilla saw it as a giant "supermarket" where they could hunt and gather all that they needed for food and medicine. To supplement their diets the Cahuilla grew plants like corn, squash, and beans in the rich desert soil. Although they were not technologically advanced by white standards, the Cahuilla led a good life, with plenty of time for songs and games. And—like most American Indians—at the heart of their life was a deep spiritual heritage.

The Cahuilla first encountered Spanish explorers in the early 19th century. However, their traditional life was not seriously disturbed until California became part of the United States. In 1853 American surveyors began laying the route for a railroad through the Coachella Valley. Ten years later the Cahuilla were devastated by a smallpox epidemic brought by the whites. The U.S. government established reservations in 1877, and by 1891 the government closely supervised almost every aspect of Cahuilla life.

Ruby Modesto was born in 1913 on the Martinez Reservation in the southern Coachella Valley. Her father was a member of the Dog Clan, one of the extended family groups that formed the basis of Desert Cahuilla social structure. Modesto later explained that her clan received its name "because the men were good hunters, like dogs always bringing something home to eat." Her mother was of a neighboring tribe called the Serrano. As a young girl, Ruby only spoke the language of the Desert Cahuilla. Then when she was 10 years old, she went to school and learned English and other subjects of the white American world.

Although Ruby was born during the reservation period, she had a direct connection to the traditional Cahuilla way of life through her father's family. Her grandfather, Francisco, was a clan chief called a *net*, who preserved the clan's history, customs, and ceremonial songs. The net lived in or next to the "Big House," which was the center of clan ceremonial activities. He was also in charge of the *kiva*, an underground chamber for meditation and councils. By the time Ruby was born, only one kiva was still in use among the Cahuilla—the kiva of her grandfather, Francisco.

When she was a young girl, Ruby's grandfather taught her about *Umna'ah*, the Creator of the Cahuilla. "He lives with us, but you can't see him. He takes care of us. Everything we have or do, He takes care of it." Francisco told Ruby to pray to Umna'ah by going alone to a quiet, beautiful place in the mountains. "He said I should talk out everything," she recalled, "say whatever I felt or needed, and then listen for an answer. That's the secret: to listen."

Along with his role as net, Francisco was a powerful medicine men or shaman, called a *pul*. A Cahuilla pul had great power to dream and to heal. Depending upon his specific powers, he could fly out of his body in spirit form, control the weather, bewitch people, or drive out evil spirits. In traditional Cahuilla society, the net worked with the puls as a governing council, meeting in the kiva to discuss problems facing the people and to pass judgment on wrongdoers.

Ruby's Uncle Charlie was also a powerful pul. He explained to her that "a real pul is born, destined to be one. It's a calling. You are chosen by Umna'ah, our Creator. He makes you a pul in the womb."

Although Cahuilla puls were usually men, Ruby Modesto was destined to be a pul and to carry on the spiritual practices of her people. The power of a pul comes from a dream helper called an *ally*. Traditionally, Cahuilla boys and some girls found their ally through using a vision-inducing plant called datura or jimson-weed. However, Modesto encountered her ally at the age of 10 through an extraordinary process of deep dreaming. (In Modesto's retelling of this experience, the word *Dreaming* is capitalized to distinguish a deep, spiritual level of Dreaming from ordinary dreaming. Spiritual *Seeing* and *Hearing* are also capitalized.)

> I Dreamed to the 13th level. The way you do that is by remembering to tell yourself to go to sleep in your 1st level ordinary dream. You consciously tell yourself to lay down and go to sleep. Then you dream a second dream. This is the 2nd level and the prerequisite for real Dreaming . . . During Dreaming the soul goes out of the body, so you have to be careful.
>
> When I dreamed to the 13th level that first time, I was young and didn't know how to get back. Usually I only dream to the 2nd or 3rd levels. But that time I kept having different dreams and falling asleep and going to another dream level. That was where I met my helper, *Ahswit,* the eagle.

Because she was young and inexperienced in the Dreaming process, Modesto's soul became lost in her dream and she slept for several days in a comalike state. When her father was unable to wake her, he called for Uncle Charlie to come and help. Each pul has certain specialties, and Uncle Charlie was an expert at healing soul loss. He brought Ruby's soul back into her body and made her promise not to Dream so deeply until she knew how to return her own soul to her body.

Although she found her ally at an early age, Modesto did not come into her full power as a pul until she was a grown woman, after the death of her mother. Before that she was a practicing Christian for many years. But as she journeyed deeper into the world of Cahuilla shamanism, she realized that she had to make a choice.

> Now I know that you cannot be a Christian and a pul. You have to choose between them, because Christians teach that a pul gets power from the devil and I don't believe that way. Of course power can be used for evil. A pul can kill or make people sick, or manipulate them against their will. A pul can make you fall in love with the ugliest person! So every pul has to choose between good and evil. The power can be used either way. I, myself, would never take a path that would hurt someone else. It's my choice everyday to use the power in a way that is helpful. And I say that the power of a pul, the Dream Helper, comes from Umna'ah. This is our ancient religion and much like the old and new testaments in which the spiritual helpers, angels, were sent to guide powerful medicine men like Moses and Jesus. Everything comes from Umna'ah.

Modesto's own specialty as a pul was healing people who were possessed by demons. Although she recognized that a modern psychotherapist would consider demonic possession "nonsense," Modesto claimed that she could actually See demons through spiritual vision and cast them out with the power of Umna'ah. And unlike a modern psychotherapist, Modesto charged nothing for her services because all her needs were provided by the Creator.

Sometimes Modesto used herbs in her healing ceremonies, and the knowledge of sacred plants formed an important part of Cahuilla shamanism. Modesto believed that plants and animals had spirits, just as human beings did. "You can talk to the plants," she said. "You really can. I don't mean you just walk up to a plant and say, 'hey bush!' But I mean be sincere. Be humble. The plants are like friends. Some of them have powerful spirits."

Modesto married and had three children, but though she led a "normal" family life in many ways, her path as a pul separated her from other people. "My husband, David, is my companion," she explained. "But I'm not bound to him. I'm alone. Since I went into shamanism, I depend on Umna'ah for everything. I pray and give thanks. We are put here to enjoy life. I bind myself to Him and ask Him to walk with me each day."

In the fall of 1976, an anthropology student named Guy Mount heard about Ruby Modesto while researching the medicinal herbs used by southern California Indians during childbirth. Modesto's aunt told Mount about her own experiences with childbirth and suggested that Ruby might be able to tell him even more about the plants. Mount was eager to meet Modesto but perplexed by the vague directions to her house. All he knew was that she lived in the desert near the Martinez Reservation and that he was supposed to drive in that direction, turn left, and then "maybe" a man on horseback would show him the way to Modesto's house. Mount later described his doubts and confusion:

> I sincerely thought driving south into the intense heat of Coachella Valley and looking for a man on horseback would be a wild goose chase. But my thoughts were a worthless barrier to discovery . . . I had to clear my mind through meditation, and trust that I would be guided on a path that was mysterious in nature. So a few days later I followed the directions to Ruby's house by driving 12 miles south of Indio to the reservation area, turning left and encountering a man on horseback! He readily pointed out the Modesto driveway and I found Ruby sitting with her husband, David, in the shade of their ramada.

Thus began a friendship and collaboration between Ruby Modesto and Guy Mount that led to a book called *Not for Innocent Ears: Spiritual Traditions of a Desert Cahuilla Medicine Woman.* The book includes the story of Modesto's life as a pul, as well as Desert Cahuilla traditions, stories, and history. The title of the book reflects the traditional attitude of most Indian shamans that the secrets of their spiritual powers are not meant for non-Indians, but only for those who are ready to Hear.

Modesto believed that times had changed and that perhaps some non-Indians would benefit from her experiences. Along with the book with Guy Mount, she coauthored an article in an anthropology journal, provided information to other anthropologists, and lectured at local colleges. At the same time, she worked to preserve her traditions among her own people by teaching Cahuilla language classes at the Martinez Reservation.

Ruby Modesto. Photograph by Guy Mount for the cover of Modesto's autobiography, Not for Innocent Ears. (Sweetlight Books, California)

Although Modesto believed that the time was right to pass on her spiritual knowledge to the non-Indian world, she knew that most white people would not accept her stories as true. "Very few white people know how to See," she explained, "nor are they willing to learn. It's too bad, because I think our vision is true and these healing methods would be used to help many people, Indians and non-Indians alike. We all have a soul, and what's true for Indians is true for other people too . . . whether they believe it or not."

Ruby Modesto died on April 7, 1980. One of her final requests was that *Not for Innocent Ears* be printed "as is," the true story of a Desert Cahuilla medicine woman. Guy Mount published the book shortly after Modesto's death, and thousands of readers have shared her story in the succeeding years. For some it is primarily a work of anthropology that helps us understand the traditional life of the Desert Cahuilla people. But for others the book is a doorway into a magical world of spiritual powers—a world that waits for those who have ears to Hear and eyes to See.

SELECTED ANNOTATED BIBLIOGRAPHY

◆ ◆ ◆

General Sources

Dockstader, Frederick J. *Great North American Indians: Profiles in Leadership.* New York: Van Nostrand Reinhold Co., 1977. A general reference book written by an Indian scholar; contains short profiles of almost every leader covered in this book, as well as profiles of many other Indian leaders.

Hirschfelder, Arlene, and Paulette Molin. *The Encyclopedia of Native American Religions.* New York: Facts On File, 1992. A general reference book on the Indian spiritual world; includes short profiles of almost every leader profiled in this book, as well as articles on many Indian religious ceremonies, festivals, beliefs, and so on.

Lamar, Howard R., ed. *The Reader's Encyclopedia of the American West.* New York: Harper & Row, 1977. An excellent general reference book on the West, with many articles on Indian leaders, tribes, treaties, battles, and so on. Most of the articles are accurate, but a few (notably "Ghost Dance") do not reflect recent research.

Mooney, James. *The Ghost Dance Religion and Wounded Knee.* New York: Dover Publications, Inc., 1973. An unabridged republication of "The Ghost-Dance Religion and the Sioux Outbreak of 1890," an Accompanying Paper to the *Fourteenth Annual Report (Part 2) of the Bureau of Ethnology,* originally published Washington, D.C.: Government Printing Office, 1896. The most important single source on pre–20th-century Indian spiritual movements; contains information on Popé, Neolin, Tenskwatawa, Kenekuk, Smohalla, John Slocum, Wovoka, Kicking Bear, and Short Bull. Too scholarly for young readers.

Sturtevant, William, gen. ed. *Handbook of North American Indians.* 9 vols. to date. Washington, D.C.: Smithsonian Institution Press, 1978– . The scholarly articles are excellent but too difficult for young readers. Many articles were consulted for this book; the most important are listed under the specific subjects below.

Trafzer, Clifford E., ed. *American Indian Prophets.* Newcastle, CA: Sierra Oaks Publishing Co., 1986. A collection of scholarly articles; includes an excellent introduction, as well as articles on Kenekuk, Smohalla, and Wovoka, and the Shakers of northern California.

Waldman, Carl. *Atlas of the North American Indian.* Maps and illustrations by Molly Braun. New York: Facts On File, 1985. A general reference book that combines geography, history, and culture; contains some good information on Indian religious movements.

———.Who Was Who in Native American History. New York: Facts On File, 1990. A general reference book with over 1,000 alphabetical listings; contains short profiles of almost every spiritual leader covered in this book.

Introduction

Drake, Samuel Gardner. *The Book of the Indians; or Biography and History of the Indians of North America from its first discovery to the year 1841*, 8th edition. First edition published 1832 as *Indian Biography*. 8th edition published Boston: Antiquarian Bookstore, 1841. Reprint New York: AMS Press, 1976. A classic book by a 19th-century historian who was reasonably accurate and sympathetic toward the Indians in general but lacked understanding of spiritual leaders.

The San Diego Union-Tribune. June 4–5, 1993. Front-page articles on the 1993 epidemic and the spiritual efforts of the Navajo medicine men.

Also see Hirshfelder/Molin, Mooney, and Trafzer under General Sources, and DeMallie under Black Elk.

Passaconaway

Bonfanti, Leo. *Biographies and Legends of the New England Indians.* Four vol. Wakefield, MA: Pride Publications, 1970–72. A readable account of relations between the early English colonists and the New England Indians; information on Passaconaway in vol. 1 (pp. 47, 52–53, 61) and vol. 3 (pp.17–20).

Day, Gordon M. "Western Abenaki." In *Handbook of North American Indians.* Vol. 7, *Northeast.* Washington, D.C.: Smithsonian Institution

Press, 1979. A scholarly article that includes brief information about Passaconaway.

Hubbard, Rev. William. *The History of the Indian Wars in New England from the First Settlement to the Termination of the War with King Philip in 1677.* Originally published 1677. Revised and edited by Samuel G. Drake. Roxbury, MA: W. Elliot Woodward, 1865. Reprinted New York: Kraus Reprint Co., 1969. Contains Passaconaway's farewell speech (p. 48).

Thatcher, Benjamin Bussey. *Indian Biography: or An Historical Account of Those Individuals Who Have Been Distinguished Among the North American Natives As Orators, Warriors, Statesmen, and Other Remarkable Characters.* Two vol. Glorieta, NM: The Rio Grande Press, Inc., 1973. Originally published New York: A. L. Fowle, 1832. Volume 1 contains a chapter on Passaconaway; the early–19th-century style is too difficult for young readers.

Winthrop, John. *Winthrop's Journal "History of New England" 1630–1649.* Two vols., edited by James Kendall Hosmer. New York: Barnes & Noble, Inc., 1959. Originally published by Charles Scribner's Sons, 1908. The journal of Governor John Winthrop of the Massachusetts Bay Colony; contains a number of references to Passaconaway, listed under "Passaconamy" in the index at the end of volume II. The 17th-century language is difficult, but young readers might find it interesting to read a short passage.

Also see Drake under Introduction.

Popé

Bancroft, Hubert Howe. *History of Arizona and New Mexico, 1530–1888.* San Francisco: The History Company, Publishers, 1889. A scholarly account that quotes many original sources on the Pueblo rebellion; too difficult for young readers. This book was actually written by Henry L. Oak, Bancroft's librarian.

Sando, Joe S. *The Pueblo Indians.* San Francisco: The Indian Historian Press, 1976. An excellent general book written by a Pueblo historian; Sando assigns less importance to Popé than most historians do.

————. "The Pueblo Revolt." In *Handbook of North American Indians*. Vol. 9, *Southwest* (Pueblo peoples). Washington, D.C.: Smithsonian Institution Press, 1980. A fine, scholarly overview of the revolt, including information drawn from Pueblo oral history.

Silverberg, Robert. *The Pueblo Revolt*. New York: Weybright and Talley, 1970. A well-written book that is clear enough for young readers.

Terrell, John Upton. *Pueblos, Gods, and Spaniards*. New York: The Dial Press, 1973. A comprehensive account of the Pueblo-Spanish conflict; well-written, but some of Terrell's details do not agree with those of more scholarly researchers.

Neolin (The Delaware Prophet)

Tanner, Helen Hornbeck, ed. *Atlas of Great Lakes Indian History*. (The Civilization of the American Indian series, vol. 174.) Norman, OK: University of Oklahoma Press, 1987. A general source that contains good information on Pontiac's Rebellion.

Also see Chapter 2, "The Delaware Prophet and Pontiac," in *The Ghost Dance Religion and Wounded Knee* by James Mooney. Listed under General Sources.

Handsome Lake

Deardorff, Merle H. "The Religion of Handsome Lake: Its Origin and Development." *Bureau of American Ethnology Bulletin* 149:77–107. Reprinted in *An Iroquois Source Book*, vol. 3, *Medicine Society Rituals*. Elizabeth Tooker, ed. New York: Garland Publishing, Inc., 1986. A scholarly article that includes some information not found in the Wallace book (below).

Wallace, Anthony F. C. *The Death and Rebirth of the Seneca*. New York: Knopf, 1970. An excellent scholarly book that is clear enough for some young readers.

————. "Origins of the Longhouse Religion." In *Handbook of North American Indians*. Vol. 15, *Northeast*. Washington, D.C.: Smithsonian Institution Press, 1979. A scholarly article that summarizes some of the key information from Wallace's book.

Tenskwatawa

Drake, Benjamin. *Life of Tecumseh, and of His Brother The Prophet; with a Historical Sketch of the Shawanoe Indians.* Cincinnati: Anderson, Gates & Wright, 1858. Reprint New York: Kraus Reprint Co., 1969. The story of Tecumseh and Tenskwatawa, written by a white scholar who interviewed some of the Indians who knew the brothers. Drake's attitude is very positive toward Tecumseh but negative toward the Prophet.

Edmunds, R. David. *The Shawnee Prophet.* Lincoln, NE: University of Nebraska Press, 1983. A scholarly biography that takes a more positive attitude toward Tenskwatawa and his leadership qualities than earlier biographies; too difficult for young readers.

Also see Mooney under General Sources.

Kenekuk

Gibson, A. M. *The Kickapoos: Lords of the Middle Border.* Norman, OK: University of Oklahoma Press, 1963. A readable book on the history of the Kickapoo tribe, but some ideas are disputed by later scholars; contains good information on Kenekuk.

Herring, Joseph B. *Kenekuk, the Kickapoo Prophet.* Lawrence, KS: University Press of Kansas, 1988. A fascinating, well-written book that is both scholarly and clear enough for some young readers.

Also see Mooney under General Sources.

Smohalla

Relander, Click. *Drummers and Dreamers.* Caldwell, ID: The Caxton Printers, 1956. Relander befriended Smohalla's nephew, Puck Hyah Toot, who was called "The Last Prophet." Relander's account of Smohalla and the Dreamer religion is poetic and authentic, but the chronology of Smohalla's life is very confusing. Advanced young readers might enjoy the traditional "storytelling" style of this book.

Also see Mooney and Trafzer under General Sources.

John Slocum

Amoss, Pamela T. "The Indian Shaker Church." In *Handbook of North American Indians*. Vol. 7, *Northwest Coast*. Washington, D.C.: Smithsonian Institution Press, 1990. A scholarly article that carries Barnett's work (below) up to the late 1980s.

Barnett, H. G. *Indian Shakers: A Messianic Cult of the Pacific Northwest*. Carbondale, IL: Southern Illinois University Press, 1957. Barnett interviewed many Shakers in 1942, including some who knew John Slocum personally. An excellent scholarly book that is too difficult for young readers.

Also see Mooney under General Sources.

Zotom

Peterson, Karen Daniels. *Plains Indian Art From Fort Marion*. (The Civilization of the American Indian Series, vol. 101.) Norman, OK: University of Oklahoma Press, 1971. A fascinating book that includes biographies of Zotom and other major artists, along with samples of their work in both color and black and white reproductions.

Wovoka

Bailey, Paul. *Wovoka: The Indian Messiah*. Los Angeles: Westernlore Press, 1957. The first full-length biography of Wovoka; clear enough for younger readers, but some facts and ideas have been proven wrong by later scholars. Bailey also wrote a fictional version of Wovoka's life entitled *Ghost Dance Messiah* (Westernlore Press, 1970).

Hittman, Michael. *Wovoka and the Ghost Dance*. Carson City, NV: Grace Dangberg Foundation, 1990. Distributed by The Yerington Paiute Tribe, Yerington, Nevada. The most complete and accurate account of Wovoka's life; also includes source material such as government correspondence and personal remembrances. Hittman compiled this book as part of a project commemorating the 100th anniversary of Wovoka's Great Revelation. Too scholarly for young readers.

Johnson, Edward C. *Walker River Paiutes: A Tribal History*. Shurz, NV: Walker River Paiute Tribe, 1975. Contains a short chapter on the Ghost Dance Prophets that emphasizes Wovoka as following directly in the steps of Wodziwob; very readable.

Jorgensen, Joseph G. "Ghost Dance, Bear Dance, and Sun Dance." In *Handbook of North American Indians*. Vol. 11, *Great Basin*. Washington, D.C.: Smithsonian Institution Press, 1986. Contains good information on the Ghost Dance of Wodziwob; less on Wovoka's Ghost Dance.

Miller, David Humphreys. *Ghost Dance*. New York: Duell, Sloan and Pearce, 1959. The story of the Lakota Ghost Dance told by a white historian who was adopted by Black Elk and interviewed Indians who participated in the dance; information on Wovoka is not accurate.

Smith, Rex Alan. *Moon of Popping Trees*. New York: Reader's Digest Press, 1975. A history of the Lakota Ghost Dance and Wounded Knee; presents both Indian and white points of view accurately and objectively; information on Wovoka is not accurate.

Also see Mooney and Trafzer under General Sources.

Black Elk

Black Elk. *The Sacred Pipe: Black Elk's Account of the Seven Rites of the Oglala Sioux*. Recorded and edited by Joseph Epes Brown. Originally published Norman, OK: University of Oklahoma Press, 1953. Paperback published New York: Penguin Books, 1971. Contains only brief information about Black Elk's life but provides insight into his thinking and the traditional beliefs of his people.

DeMallie, Raymond J., ed. *The Sixth Grandfather: Black Elk's Teachings Given to John G. Neihardt*. Lincoln, NE: University of Nebraska Press, 1984. The original transcripts of Black Elk's sessions with Neihardt in 1931 and 1944; also includes an excellent biographical introduction by DeMallie, emphasizing Black Elk's later life as a Roman Catholic; all quotations from Black Elk in the profile are taken from these original transcripts. Too difficult for young readers.

Neihardt, John G. *Black Elk Speaks: Being the Life Story of a Holy Man of the Oglala Sioux*. Originally published New York: William Morrow

& Co., 1932. Republished Lincoln, NE: University of Nebraska Press, 1961. Paperback edition New York: Pocket Books, 1972. Some scholars argue that this book contains too much of Neihardt's own thinking; however, after comparing it with the original transcripts, DeMallie (above) concluded that it preserves the most important aspects of Black Elk's teachings. Neihardt's writing ability makes this a delightful, readable book that is highly recommended for young readers.

Mountain Wolf Woman

Mountain Wolf Woman. *Mountain Wolf Woman, Sister of Crashing Thunder: The Autobiography of a Winnebago Indian.* Edited by Nancy Oestreich Lurie. Ann Arbor, MI: The University of Michigan Press, 1961. Ann Arbor Paperback edition, 1966. Mountain Wolf Woman's narrative is fascinating and readable; however, the significance and chronology of the events is confusing without constant reference to Lurie's excellent notes.

Ruby Modesto

Modesto, Ruby, and Guy Mount. *Not for Innocent Ears: Spiritual Traditions of a Desert Cahuilla Medicine Woman.* Arcata, CA: Sweetlight Books (mailing address: 16625 Heitman Road, Cottonwood, California 96022), 1980. The heart of the book is the "Autobiography of a Pul" told in Modesto's own words and clear enough for younger readers; other chapters cover Desert Cahuilla history, traditions, and stories. Mount also offers a suggested high school/junior college curriculum for a unit of study entitled "Our Indian Heritage."

INDEX

Boldface type indicates main headings.
Italic type indicates illustrations.